THE BLUE STREAKS & LITTLE GIANTS

MORE THAN A CENTURY OF
SANDUSKY & FREMONT ROSS FOOTBALL

VINCE GUERRIERI

Charleston   London

THE
History
PRESS

Published by The History Press
Charleston, SC 29403
www.historypress.net

First published 2013

Manufactured in the United States

ISBN 978.1.60949.991.4

Library of Congress CIP data applied for.

CONTENTS

ACKNOWLEDGEMENTS

I came to Fremont to be the sports editor for the *News-Messenger* in 2005—just in time for the 100th meeting (well, as further research revealed, the 101st meeting but the 100th regular-season meeting) of Ross and Sandusky. That fall, I wrote a five-part series detailing the rivalry. In researching that, I talked at some length with two men: Rob Lytle and Daniel H. Lease. Rob knew a thing or two about rivalries. After playing for Ross, he went to the University of Michigan, where he partook in the ten-year war between Bo Schembechler and Woody Hayes. One night at a Ross Hall of Fame dinner, Rob told me a story about how Bo asked him to switch from tailback to fullback. He wasn't the worse for wear, finishing his career as an all-American and third in the Heisman voting, but the story left me in stitches, and I can't do it justice. After college, he played for the Denver Broncos, which at the time had many pitched battles in the AFC West with the Raiders.

Dan Lease was also a Ross alumnus. He went on to some success in the business world in the Fremont area and served on his alma mater's school board. He could remember back to the days when the Little Giants and Blue Streaks met on Thanksgiving, and when the swimming pool at the school on Croghan Street was state-of-the-art (by the time I got there, it was decrepit, for lack of a better word). As I continued to research this book, his name kept popping up. He had done tremendous research on Ross football and made this project a little easier. Both men are gone now, but I owe them profound thanks.

ACKNOWLEDGEMENTS

My boss, Jill Nevels-Haun, and my co-workers at the *News-Messenger* were all wonderful and supportive as I undertook this project. My friend, former *Sandusky Register* sports editor Dan Angelo, and current sports editor Mark Hazelwood also helped me in my research, as did *Register* chief photographer Jason Werling and Rusty Miller, the Associated Press sports editor for Ohio.

Fremont City School superintendent Traci McCaudy was supportive of the project, and athletic director Chad Berndt opened up the hall of fame room for me to find a treasure trove of information.

Obviously, I came into this project knowing more about Fremont's side of the rivalry than I did about Sandusky's. The one person I kept getting pointed to for all things Blue Streaks was Gene Kidwell. He more than lived up to his billing, providing information, resources and photos for this book.

I did a lot of research at Birchard Public Library, the library at the Rutherford B. Hayes Presidential Center, and the Sandusky Library. Ron Davidson in Sandusky helped me acquire some of the photos used in this book through their collection, and Nan Card and Gil Gonzalez were similarly helpful with the Hayes Center's collection. Support your local libraries.

The Hayes Center and the Sandusky Library also helped provide photos for the book, as did innumerable other sources, including people associated with both programs and sports information directors from throughout the Midwest. I owe them all profound thanks, so pay attention to the photo credits.

I'd also like to thank all the people who were willing to share their stories from this rivalry. Their names are listed in the reference section at the back of the book.

And last but not least, I couldn't do this without my family, including my parents, Chuck and Rose, and my brother, Adam. My lovely wife, Shannon, proves every day that when it comes to marriage, I have really outkicked my coverage, and her parents, Tony and Linda Carilli, helped take care of our daughter, Sammy, so I could devote my full attention to the book.

CHAPTER 1

The Pep Rally

A League Title, a Playoff Spot and 115 Years of Honor and History

October 27, 2010, was a rainy night at the Sandusky County Fairgrounds. At one point, the fairgrounds had been the home field for the Fremont High School football team, but they'd played almost eighty-five years on the site now occupied by Don Paul Stadium, a shimmering new grandstand with a FieldTurf field that was the envy of many high schools in northwest Ohio.

Among the games played at the fairgrounds were matchups against Sandusky High School. The Fremont High School football team's first game was against Sandusky in 1895, and the two teams had played each year since 1906—with just five exceptions.

That night, the fairgrounds were the site of a pep rally in anticipation of the 105th matchup between the Fremont Ross Little Giants (their nickname was bestowed admiringly after a Fremont upset win over Sandusky in 1925) and the Sandusky Blue Streaks.

Pep rallies in Fremont weren't uncommon before Sandusky games (neither were pep rallies in Sandusky before Fremont games); only the location changed. Previously, it had been an annual occurrence on the steps of the Sandusky County Courthouse (Fremont is the seat of Sandusky County; Sandusky is in Erie County). Every year, there were pride and bragging rights at stake. This year, for the first time in a while, both teams were battling for a league title and a possible playoff spot. It was also the last year for their league, the Greater Buckeye Conference, marking the second time in twenty-five years that the Ross-Sandusky game would decide a conference winner in the conference's last year.

Ross players who were around the previous year were smarting at the recollection of a 30–0 shutout at Strobel Field, which like Don Paul Stadium had been used for many years. As if they needed more motivation, Ross trotted out the old football heroes.

There was Tony Gant, who was the Columbus Touchdown Club's Mr. Football and who also went on to play defensive back for the University of Michigan. Gant was living in Sylvania, where his son Allen (who would also play football at Michigan) was part of a state championship football team at Southview, but Fremont and Ross remained in his heart.

John Lewis, a 1952 Ross graduate who went on to play in two Rose Bowls for Michigan State, also spoke. Lewis was a running back on unstoppable Ross teams of the 1950s, when he acquired the nickname "Big Thunder" for his punishing running style, complementing the speed and quickness of Jerome Surratt, who was nicknamed "Little Thunder." Lewis played in the Canadian Football League and turned down a baseball contract from the Pittsburgh Pirates. Big Thunder, a Michigan State graduate, lived near East Lansing but made it a point to come down and speak.

Shawn Simms, an all–Mid American Conference linebacker and assistant coach throughout college football, was also there. Simms was the first Ross athlete to letter in four sports. He went on to letter in football at Bowling Green State University and bounced around as an assistant football coach, with stops at San Diego State, Iowa State, Illinois, Miami of Ohio, Heidelberg and Ohio State University.

Aaron Opelt also spoke. He was the only speaker not in his alma mater's hall of fame—and that's only because he wasn't that long out of high school. The Ross hall came calling for Opelt in his first year of eligibility in 2013, after he graduated from the University of Toledo, where he started at quarterback for the Rockets as a freshman. He was under center when UT went to Ann Arbor and beat the Wolverines in the Big House. Opelt actually got more offers to play college baseball, but football's siren song was too much for him to resist.

But the most animated speaker was Rob Lytle, a Ross graduate who had gone on to play running back for Bo Schembechler at Michigan and had played for the Denver Broncos in the NFL. Lytle returned to his hometown after his playing career was over and had become a pillar of the community. He loved Fremont Ross football enough that he could still be spotted on the chain gang at Little Giants games. He saw it as a point of pride that the rivalry between Ross and Sandusky, thoroughly dominated by the Blue Streaks through the 1960s, turned in Ross's favor once he got to high school. And he could be counted on to rile up the hometown crowd for what he thought was the best high school rivalry in Ohio—a state that can claim to be the cradle of football.

Lytle's body failed him during his too-brief NFL career, and he had a stroke on New Year's Eve 2008, but he was up, around and seemingly ready to put the pads on himself as he told stories about his mother, a Sandusky native, who would make it a point to needle her son before the Little Giants matched up with the Blue Streaks. And he whipped the crowd into a frenzy by mentioning the condescension of their rivals to the northeast.

"They think we should still be called Lower Sandusky!" Lytle yelled.

But it was Opelt who put the game into perspective. The game held special significance for him, as it did for all Ross players. His parents had told him that the week before the Sandusky game, he seemed different—like a switch had been flipped. As Ross quarterback, Opelt led the Little Giants to a total of nine wins. The last was the 100th regular season meeting between the Blue Streaks and Little Giants, at Strobel Field. Opelt, a high school quarterback who could make opposing defensive coordinators sweat when he was scrambling in the backfield as the pocket collapsed on third and long, had taken hold of every quarterback record in that 2005 Ross-Sandusky game, a 42–20 Little Giants win. It was the only game Opelt would win against Sandusky.

"That rivalry will mean everything to you," Opelt told the crowd. "It's where legends are made."

CHAPTER 2

ORIGINS

S andusky began as a French outpost in 1750, in the days before Ohio was a state and the United States was a country, when northwest Ohio was a wilderness lined with Native Americans, and British and French forces fought for supremacy in the new world. The fort transferred to British hands and ultimately became part of Connecticut. The Nutmeg State laid claim to land up to 120 miles west of the western border of Pennsylvania, north of the Forty-first parallel and south of Lake Erie, for soldiers who helped fight for American independence during the Revolution. The land was called the Connecticut Western Reserve, a name that still can be found in northeast Ohio. Most of the land was sold to speculators, but a total of 500,000 acres—mostly what are now Erie and Huron Counties—was held back with the intention of giving it to Connecticut residents who lost their land and property in the Revolution. Because most of those losses came when the British burned property, they became known as the Firelands—another name that remains to this day. After Connecticut settlers ceded the land to Ohio (one of the townships in the area was named for a city in Connecticut, Danbury), the lands were formed into Huron County in 1809, six years after Ohio became the first state formed out of the Northwest Territory.

What is now Fremont was the site of Fort Stephenson, an outpost on the Sandusky River during the early days of statehood for Ohio. In 1813, as British forces were marching through what is now northwest Ohio and southwest Michigan in the western front of the War of 1812, they were repelled at Fort Meigs in what is now Perrysburg. They marched on to Fort

Stephenson, commanded by Major George Croghan, who was ordered by U.S. general William Henry Harrison to abandon the fort. Croghan refused and held off British forces with "Old Betsy," a Spanish cannon captured by the British and then captured by colonists in the Revolutionary War.

After the War of 1812, Old Betsy went to the Allegheny Arsenal in Lawrenceville (now a neighborhood in Pittsburgh), and it was requested by what was then called Lower Sandusky, the town that had grown up around the site of the fort. (The town was so called because it was situated on the lower Sandusky River, the same reason a town south of it is called Upper Sandusky.) The cannon went to Sandusky by mistake, where it was buried in a barn. Some residents of Lower Sandusky went to Sandusky under cover of night, dug the cannon out and spirited it back to its rightful home. Today, the cannon sits on the lawn of Birchard Public Library, on the hill where Fort Stephenson used to be—not far from the final resting place of George Croghan, who was dug up from his family estate in Kentucky and reinterred on the hill outside of the library in 1906.

In 1824, the city of Sandusky was incorporated, becoming an inland port and shipbuilding center on Lake Erie. In 1838, Huron County split, and Erie County formed around Sandusky. Also that year, the first school directors for the city were elected. By 1845, no fewer than three schools had been built in the city. Sandusky was one of the first cities in Ohio with a high school, graduating its first class of four in 1855. A new high school, which later became Adams Junior High School, was built in 1869 after the old one caught fire.

Sandusky's roots as a resort town go back to 1882, but in 1889, George Boeckling formed the Cedar Point Pleasure Resort Company. Three years later, the beachside resort got its first roller coaster, the Switchback Railway, which stood twenty-five feet tall and took riders on a thrill ride with top speeds of ten miles per hour. By 1897, Boeckling's company had controlling interest in the park, which would become a destination for roller coaster fans and people looking for a vacation at a beach resort.

In 1849, Lower Sandusky was renamed Fremont for John C. Fremont, a Mexican War veteran and former California military governor then exploring the West. In 1850, a school system was developed, and a new brick building was erected at the corner of Garrison Street and Park Avenue. That brick building would be replaced by what was called the Central School at the same site in 1891. In 1864, Clyde school superintendent W.W. Ross was elected superintendent of Fremont schools, a role he filled until his death in 1906. His son Will D. Ross finished the remainder of his term.

Among those who returned to Fremont after the Civil War was a lawyer who had risen to the rank of general, Rutherford B. Hayes. Many other veterans returned to home lives in small towns and cities throughout Ohio and the United States, taking with them new knowledge and traditions. Confederate prisoners of war at Johnson's Island—in Ottawa County, not far from Fremont or Sandusky—played a game called "base ball," and clubs sprung up throughout northern Ohio after the Civil War. In 1869, the Cincinnati Red Stockings hired players from other cities and paid them, becoming the first professional baseball team.

But while baseball grew up in cities, a different game was taking hold at colleges. Also in 1869, the first American football game was played in New Jersey, with Rutgers beating Princeton 6–4. The game spread to colleges up and down the East Coast and eventually moved inland. It was also taken up by high schools.

On October 25, 1890, the first high school football game was played in Ohio, with the Cleveland University School blanking Cleveland Central High 20–0. Technically, Cleveland Central was the only high school in the game, since the University School was regarded as a prep school at that point. Two years later, Pudge Heffelfinger became the first professional football player when he signed a $500 contract with the Allegheny Athletic Association in Pittsburgh. Football had become a spectator sport, with games being played on the scholastic, collegiate and professional levels. But it particularly would take hold in Ohio, where a Cleveland native named John Heisman was coaching college football at Oberlin and Buchtel (now the University of Akron).

In 1894, C.J. Strobel was elected to the Sandusky School Board. He remains the youngest person ever elected to the board and also the longest-serving school board member. He would be the namesake for the Sandusky football stadium. Also that year, Canton and Massillon high schools met for the first time on the football field. The two Stark County high schools would form the longest continuous football rivalry in Ohio. Both became powerhouses in the sport—by reputation if not always by deed—and cast a long shadow over Ohio high school football.

In 1895, Edgerton "Johnny" Garvin arrived in Fremont from Annapolis, Maryland, home of the U.S. Naval Academy. While in Annapolis, Garvin saw midshipmen playing rugby on the fields there.

Garvin is literally the man who brought football to Fremont. In fact, he brought a football and organized a team, the second athletic team at Fremont High School after the track team started in 1892.

In those days before high school sports were policed by the Ohio High School Athletic Association (OHSAA), when high school membership itself was a little more fluid, Garvin not only coached the team but also played quarterback. A newspaper account looking back from the 1960s talked about how primitive the game was at the time: "Funds to equip the team were few; boys had to provide their own suits, pay their own bills, dress at home and clean their own uniforms. Although tickets were sold during football's infancy here, many persons were admitted to games free, and 'pass the hat' was a common sight."

Fremont's first game took place on November 2, 1895, at the Erie County Fairgrounds (now MacArthur Park) in Sandusky, against the team from Sandusky High School.

"The high school football team of this city, which left for Sandusky Saturday morning did not return with victory on their shoulder, but nevertheless, the boys' countenances were wreathed in smiles," wrote the *Fremont Daily News*. "They went to Sandusky, put up a fine game for their first contest, and even if they did not win, they kept the score down and did some superior playing and can well feel proud of their initial game."

Sandusky won that game 6–0, with the names of the scorers lost to eternity. At the time, a touchdown was four points, and any kicked score (point after or field goal) was worth two. Details from the game were scarce, but Fremont wouldn't get its first win until the last game of the season, when the Fremont reserves shut out Flower Valley 16–0. The win over Fremont, on the other hand, was the first of eleven straight wins for Sandusky.

The two teams met again in 1896, with Sandusky riding a seven-game win streak. Fremont had won its opener 14–0 against Fostoria but lost at Clyde 10–0. Sandusky scored a touchdown in the first half to take a 6–0 lead and scored again in the second half—but not without some controversy, according to the *Fremont Daily News*: "The boys claim the ball was put in play by Sandusky before their line was formed. After a long discussion, the referee, who knew very little about football and favored the Sandusky players, gave Sandusky the point." However, the *Daily News* account said there were no hard feelings and that both teams viewed each other as competitors, not enemies. "An evidence of this kindly spirit pervading the game was seen in the generous allowance of 14 minutes instead of 3, according to rule, when full back [Hans] Stamm was injured in the pile-up," the *Daily News* reported.

Fremont would go on to finish 3–2–1, but the Streaks were undefeated and unscored upon in five games, winning a mythical state title. These were the days before playoffs, wire service polls or even the OHSAA, so the reputation of excellence meant a lot. If a team declared itself the best and had enough people who agreed with that sentiment, they could call themselves state champions.

"Sandusky now holds the pennant of the interscholastic league and claims the championship of high schools of the state," wrote the *Sandusky Register* after Sandusky finished the season with a 12–0 win over Fostoria on Thanksgiving. "Who can dispute it?"

The problem with that format—and even with the polls that replaced them—is that it wasn't decided on the field.

In 1897, Fremont and Sandusky met to open the season on October 15. Many histories of the rivalry didn't include this matchup, but Justin Millisor and Dennis Tompkins, in putting together their Fremont Ross record book, discovered it by poring over old issues of the *Fremont Daily News*. The headline was "The Fish Eaters," mocking the players from Sandusky, which had built a thriving commercial fishing industry as an inland port on the Great Lakes.

In the 1897 matchup, Fremont defeated Sandusky 18–0. The team featured the Childs brothers, Walter and Clarence. Their father, James, owned the clothing store in downtown Fremont. The *Fremont Daily News* account of the game noted that Clarence, playing halfback, "did excellent work and advanced the ball at will." But it was Garvin, Bert German and Hopple (whose first name is lost to history) who scored for Fremont. German was a principal at the high school. "The Sandusky boys conducted themselves as gentlemen and we will be pleased to have them with us again," reported the *Daily News*. Clarence Childs went on to play football and run track at Kenyon College as an undergraduate and at Yale as a law student. He won a bronze medal in athletics for his hammer throw in the 1912 Olympics, where he became friends with fellow teammate Jim Thorpe. (Childs would hire Thorpe as an assistant coach when he became football coach at Indiana University.)

The day after Fremont beat Sandusky, October 16, 1897, was the first meeting between two bitter rivals in college football, as the University of Michigan added Ohio State to its football schedule. It was a tune-up game for the Wolverines, who won 34–0. In its early years, like Ross and Sandusky, this would be a lopsided rivalry. But like Ross and Sandusky—each of which sent more than their share of players to Ann Arbor and Columbus—it would turn into a pitched rivalry and a game of great importance for both teams.

It would be another decade before Fremont and Sandusky met again on the football field. In 1904, Jim Gilliard was the first Sandusky player to be named all-Ohio. The halfback/defensive end was one of the first players from the rivalry to make his way into the Ohio State-Michigan rivalry.

The 1897 Fremont High School football team. *Bottom row, left to right*: Edgerton "Johnny" Garvin, quarterback; Clarence Childs, halfback; Irvin Hague, guard. *Second row, left to right*: Fred Marvin, end; George Grob, tackle; Walter Childs, halfback. *Back row, left to right*: Bert German, coach; Frank Hess, tackle; Charles Zartman, center; and Bert Cook, end. Johnny Garvin was the coach and played for the team. German, an administrator at the school, also played on the team. Clarence Childs would go on to win a bronze medal in the 1912 Olympics. *Photo courtesy Rutherford B. Hayes Presidential Center.*

The *Chicago Tribune* reported that there were eighteen deaths and 159 serious injuries that year attributed to football, mostly on the scholastic level. The following year, there were nineteen deaths and 137 serious injuries. Something had to be done to stem the game's lack of organization and violent formations like the flying wedge, in which players linked arms and ran down the field, forming a wall. The game had "crippled more players than were wounded in the Boer War," said the *Fremont Messenger* in what wasn't necessarily hyperbole.

The International Athletic Association of the United States was formed in 1905 with pressure from President Theodore Roosevelt, who believed in the importance of football as an athletic and character-building endeavor but wanted to make it safer. The IAAUS, which changed its name in 1910 to the National Collegiate Athletic Association, legalized use of a forward pass, meaning that a player in the backfield could throw the ball to another player running downfield.

The first forward pass was thrown by Bradbury Robinson, the quarterback for St. Louis University. It was a twenty-yard connection with Jack Schneider during a game at Carroll College on September 5, 1906. Robinson, who was born in Bellevue (about halfway between Fremont and Sandusky) but moved to St. Louis as a child, also threw the first incomplete pass, which under the rules of the day was a turnover. With turning the ball over more likely than a successful forward pass, most teams shied away from it.

Also in 1906, Fremont and Sandusky resumed their rivalry. As schedules were a little looser then, Fremont and Sandusky played twice. The first time, in Fremont, resulted in a 23–0 Sandusky win. "Before the contest started, football enthusiasts picked Fremont to win, they being much more heavier than the local team," the *Sandusky Register* wrote. "Sandusky showed wonderful speed and their interference at times was remarkable."

Sandusky followed that win up with a 22–0 win over Norwalk. Fremont played Clyde twice, winning both games, 4–0 and 5–0. At the rematch

The 1906 Sandusky High School football team. *Photo courtesy Sandusky Library.*

in Sandusky, the home team emerged victorious, 5–0, for a season sweep by Sandusky. There were talks of a third game that year between the two schools, but the *Register* reported that while Sandusky was interested, Fremont was not. Sandusky finished the season 5–0 and was unscored upon.

In 1907, Fremont and Sandusky tied 5–5, the lone blemish in a 4–0–1 season for Sandusky. According to the *Fremont Daily Messenger*, Sandusky players and partisans were particularly incensed over the outcome of the game, saying that Fremont officials had handed the score to the home team.

Also that year, what is now the Ohio High School Athletic Association met for the first time. In its nascent years, high school sports weren't well policed. It wasn't uncommon to see coaches like Garvin or administrators like German at Fremont take the field for their team, and ringers abounded. (Fremont lost a game 24–0 to Norwalk High School in 1895. Some of the Norwalk players were workers for the A.B. Chase Piano Company). Many towns—like Fremont and Sandusky—had town teams as well as school teams, but some smaller towns just had one team. In 1908, plans for a Fremont-Gibsonburg high school game fell apart when it was revealed that only one member of the Gibsonburg team was actually a high school student. Also that year, Sandusky administrators protested a Fremont player, saying that he had played for the team for four years already and thus couldn't still be a high school student.

The OHSAA also provided some structure to scheduling, which at that point was often just a matter of saying, "Do you want to get together for a game?" The first state tournament in any sport was in 1908, with a track meet at Beaver Field at Denison University in Granville. It would be almost another lifetime before the state started a football tournament.

Fremont and Sandusky met twice in 1908. In the first game, in Fremont, team captain Art Christy and Tom O'Farrell scored touchdowns to stake Fremont to a 10–0 lead. But Sandusky scored a touchdown, which the *Daily Messenger* said was allowed despite players being off side because Sandusky threatened to quit. The *Register* said the touchdown was good even though Fremont players protested that players were off side. Sandusky then scored again, this time kicking the point after to take an 11–10 lead. With two minutes left to play, Fremont was at its own forty-yard line. Fremont moved down field, with the final touchdown being scored by Harry Stout. O'Farrell's extra point made it 16–11. Sandusky drove down the field and was on the verge of scoring, the *Register* said, when time ran out. "The Sanduskians put up a game fight and would have won if the time had been extended three minutes longer," the paper wrote.

The *Messenger* said that it was Fremont's first win against Sandusky. (Throughout the rivalry's history, early dates and games have been misidentified due to spotty local coverage and spotty memories as years went on. The first game was played in 1895, but newspaper accounts throughout the rivalry have put the first matchup at 1896, 1897 and 1906. Some accounts in the 1950s said a game was played in 1905, when Fremont didn't even field a team. The final score was listed as 23–0, which was the score of the first of the two matchups in 1906.)

The two teams met again a month later, this time in Sandusky. The home team got off to a 27–0 halftime lead, but Fremont scored in the second half. With about three minutes left to play, the Sandusky fullback Holzapfel was taken down at the three but rolled over the goal line, according to the report in the *Fremont Daily Messenger*. The touchdown was allowed, and team captain Art Christy pulled the team off the field, forfeiting the game. The next day's *Sandusky Register* ran the headline, "Fremont Footballists Perform the Baby Act," adding that Sandusky was superior in all ways to Fremont. "The game proved that the Fremont team is in no way a match for Sandusky High." The *Daily News* said that Sandusky had twelve players on the field, while Fremont had only eleven. "The large score made by the fishcatchers was not made by playing a superior article of football, but the touchdowns which scored the points were in reality presented to the home players by the generosity of the official," the *Daily News* wrote. "They could play the Sandusky players to a standstill, but they could not play the Sandusky official." The *Messenger* noted, "Sandusky must be hard up for footballs, as they went south with Fremont's."

Fremont High School football team captain Art Christy pulled the team off the field in the second Fremont-Sandusky game in 1908, causing Fremont to forfeit. *Photo courtesy Jon Kerns.*

The abrupt ending of the second 1908 meeting didn't stop the two teams from meeting in 1909. "Fremont High has one of the best teams for its weight in northern Ohio and will play some of the strongest teams in the near future," the *Sandusky Register* wrote. Sandusky won 11–6 in a matchup the *Register* declared the teams' first meeting since 1907. Sexton and Helm scored for Sandusky, while Art Christy scored for Fremont. All the scoring came in the first half. "The second half was marked by much punting," the *Register* wrote. "The game was uninteresting to the spectators, as the thrilling open work play was absent."

In 1909, the Fremont school district started building a new high school on Croghan Street, across from the War of 1812 monument, Old Betsy and Croghan's earthly remains. The building, which opened in 1912, had a plaque recognizing British soldiers killed in the Battle of Fort Stephenson who had been buried in a common grave on the site.

The 1910 game was a peaceable matchup—at least, for readers of the *Register*. The Sandusky paper mentioned in its story about the Blue and White's 10–5 win that "the disputes which are usually so prominent in Fremont-Sandusky athletic contests were happily lacking." But the *Daily News* pointed out that Sandusky demonstrated cold feet and refused to play in Fremont, so the game was played in Sandusky. Oddly, the *Daily News* also said the matchup was the first time in two years that the schools had any athletic interaction of any kind, "Fremont cutting Sandusky off their list, owing to the shabby treatment always accorded the Fremont men at Sandusky."

Thompson and Dorn scored for Sandusky, while Tom O'Farrell scored for Fremont. The *Messenger* said that Sandusky partisans gathered around the Fremont team's huddle and prevented coach Dick Sherwood from giving instructions to his players. The *Messenger* also reported that some fans spit on Fremont players. "Never in the history of Fremont High School have the boys been so disgracefully treated, and it is to be hoped that all athletic relations between the two cities will be severed."

On the other hand, the *Daily News* wanted a rematch. "Sandusky High will spend the week in warming up their feet and if sufficient heat is obtained will come to Fremont next Saturday for a return game." There was no rematch.

In 1911, Sandusky formed the Northern Ohio League with Lorain, Norwalk and Elyria. The Blue and White didn't meet Fremont that year, but the following year, Fremont and Bellevue joined the league, which became known as the Little Big Six (LBS).

Photo from the 1910 Fremont-Sandusky game. *Photo courtesy Jon Kerns.*

The 1910 Fremont High School football team, helpfully wearing jerseys to identify what year the photo was taken. *Photo courtesy Jon Kerns.*

"The advent of the LBS worked wonders in Fremont scholastic grid circles," wrote *Messenger* sportswriter James O'Farrell, who went by the byline "Col. O'Farrell," in a football program years later. "Paid coaches, attention to playing fields, trained cheer leaders, bands of rooters, a high school band and, above all, uniforms, gear and comforts of a field house developed in turn."

Fremont hired a new coach, Robert Todd, a former collegiate football star at Wooster, for the 1912 season. Todd emphasized speed over size. Fans expected a beating from Sandusky in 1912, with the *Daily News* saying "not that Fremont is expected to win, the interest being in how much Fremont can stop Sandusky's onslaught." As it turned out, Fremont couldn't, getting beaten 37–0 by the Blue and White. "Sandusky greatly outweighed Fremont and found no difficulty in penetrating the local defense," wrote the *Daily News*. But the first league title was won by Lorain, which clinched the crown with a win over Norwalk the same day as the Fremont-Sandusky game.

On October 25, 1913, Fremont and Sandusky battled to a 6–6 tie. Willard Peach scored for Fremont, but in the third quarter, with Sandusky facing fourth and goal from the Fremont four-yard line, Fremont was whistled for a false start, and Ernshaw scored from two yards out for Sandusky to tie the game. Neither team could kick an extra point. The *Fremont Daily News* account described the teams as evenly matched and trying the forward pass on several occasions. "Few forward passes were worked successfully although both teams made several nice gains via the air route," it noted.

A week later, the Notre Dame football team proved the forward pass was more than a novelty during a game in New York against Army. The Cadets were 4–0 on the season, while the Irish were 3–0. Quarterback Gus Dorais threw for 243 yards and two touchdowns on fourteen-for-seventeen passing—good numbers today, but positively astounding a century ago.

"The yellow leather egg was in the air half the time, with the Notre Dame team spread out in all directions over the field waiting for it," said the next day's *New York Times*. "The Army players were hopelessly confused and chagrined before Notre Dame's great playing."

While working as lifeguards at Cedar Point in Sandusky that summer, Dorais and Knute Rockne honed their passing attack by throwing around a football on the beach. Rockne met his wife, the former Bonnie Skiles, in Sandusky as well. She was a waitress in the Grill Room. They married the following summer—also in Sandusky, with Dorais serving as best man.

Sandusky won in dominant fashion in 1914, 35–0. Fremont could muster just three first downs in the game. The Blue and White's passing attack was halted in rainy, muddy conditions, but it was no matter. "Fremont High was completely outclassed," the *Register* wrote. "The game was Sandusky's all the way."

Fremont fans were excited when Sandusky came to town in 1915 with a parade and pep rally the day before the game. The Blue and White were leading the Little Big Six. "Should Fremont win," the *Fremont Daily News* wrote, "it means she has played an important part in the conference." The *Daily News* said the team was hopeful to hold Sandusky to a low score but that their work was cut out for them, as the Blue and White had demonstrated proficiency at the forward pass.

In 1915, football players and coaches everywhere pored over the new Walter Camp Football Guide, learning new rules. It was now illegal to hit players after the whistle, which apparently had been a common enough practice that it had to be outlawed. That year, the Sandusky school building received several additions, including a gymnasium and shower room, promising state-of-the-art athletic facilities.

Fremont found itself out of the league race with a 33–3 loss to Lorain, but it could play spoiler the following week against Sandusky, which was undefeated in the Little Big Six. The Blue and White beat Fremont 36–0, the third shutout win by at least thirty-five points by Sandusky over Fremont in four years. It appeared Sandusky would end Lorain's stranglehold on the league title, clinching at least a share of the Little Big Six, but the Blue and White were forced to forfeit four games—including the win over Fremont—because of the use of ineligible players. The Little Big Six crown remained in Lorain.

The Purple and White were the first team to score a touchdown against Lorain in 1916, although they still lost 33–12 in the week before the Sandusky game. Fremont came out and beat Sandusky 19–0 for its first win in the series since 1908. Burdett Schreffler scored twice for the Purple and White, while William Fellers scored once as Fremont "pounded, battered and smashed its way through the Sandusky high line," according to the *Daily News*.

Fremont had a new coach in 1917, but it was a familiar face. Robert Todd was back coaching the Purple and White, who lost 18–0 to Sandusky. In a conspicuous bit of boosterism, even by the standards of the day, the *Fremont Daily News* said, "The boys certainly played the game of their lives and deserved to win."

The 1918 Fremont-Sandusky game was scheduled for October 19, but the game was postponed as the Spanish flu pandemic took its toll through northern Ohio. In Fremont, churches and schools closed, and the game against Lorain was canceled. Area residents took their chances in mass exposure, venturing out on November 11 to celebrate the signing of the armistice that ended the Great War. Shortly after that, the flu alert was lifted, and people started to go about their daily routines. The Sandusky game was made up on November 23, with the Blue and White prevailing 33–0. In all, the year finished ignominiously for Fremont, which went 0–6–1. Sandusky

The 1916 Fremont High School football team. *Photo courtesy Rutherford B. Hayes Presidential Center.*

finished 3–0–1 in a flu-shortened season in which the Little Big Six decreed that no championship would be awarded.

In 1919, Fremont had another new coach. Warren Vannarsdoll succeeded George Crane, who was hired as the coach at Findlay High School. Fremont was 5–0 going into the matchup with Lorain, which had won five of the previous eight league titles. The Steelmen prevailed 9–7 in a game Fremont played under protest after a 7–7 tie was broken with a Fremont safety. The next week's matchup against Sandusky was suddenly a must-win game.

Sandusky scored first, but touchdowns by Harold Boyer and John Bowlus—who played most of the game with a broken index finger—gave Fremont the lead and the win 12–6. From then on, Fremont was playing with house money.

"Even if Fremont High gridders to not happen to win the flag this season," the *Daily Messenger* wrote, "The town will not be very much disappointed. No one really had anticipated much of a football team here. Everyone became convinced that Fremont was in the Little Big Six simply because they needed someone for the cellar position."

Fans wondered if the team's winless season the year before was due to a lack of talent or lack of coaching. Fremont's 22–0 shellacking of Crane's Findlay team gave credence to the idea that it was bad coaching and allowed Fremont to stay in the driver's seat for its first Little Big Six title. In the final week of the season, more than four hundred Fremont boosters went to the Bellevue/Lorain football game. A Bellevue win would allow Fremont to win an outright league title. The Redmen upset Lorain, and Fremont hammered Norwalk the next day, 21–3, to win the Little Big Six title. Fremont finished the season with a 7–0 win over Dayton St. Mary's College—now the University of Dayton. In those days, it was not uncommon for high school teams to play small college teams. Fremont's 9–1 record was the best in school history—and the most wins in a year by the school until 1955.

Ticket from the 1919 Fremont-Sandusky football game. Although the time says 3:00 p.m., the game time was moved up to 2:30 p.m. so the game could be played in the daylight.

On September 17, 1920, a group of football club owners met in a Hupmobile dealership in Canton belonging to Ralph Hay, whose other holdings included a football team, the Canton Bulldogs. The eleven owners—including George "Papa Bear" Halas—developed a league, the American Pro Football Association. The league consisted mostly of teams in Ohio, with a few in Indiana, Illinois and New York—almost all in the Great Lakes area. The league's first president was one of its players, Jim Thorpe, arguably the most famous athlete in the United States, and Clarence Childs's former assistant at Indiana. Thorpe was initially hesitant to take the job but was convinced by Hay to take the role for the sake of the nascent league's publicity.

The new football league needed all the good will it could muster. Today, the college game serves as a de facto farm system for the NFL, but when the league was just starting, college football was more popular—and more respectable. College football was played by educated gentlemen (and college

The 1919 Fremont High School team won the Little Big Six championship. *Photo courtesy Van Ness's Time Out Sports Bar.*

education at that point was still largely limited to the middle and upper classes) who played simply for the glory of the sport. Professional football was played for money, and its players were just as likely to have come out of steel mills and coal mines as they were from college. The same year the APFA was founded, the Western Conference, which was just starting to be called the Big Ten in some publications, said that players who participated in professional games would lose their varsity letters and that any officials working pro games would be banned from the league. Also, the American Football Coaches' Association called professional football "detrimental to the best interests of American football and American youth" in 1921.

Fremont started the 1920 season with two non-league losses, a 7–0 loss in a game to Fremont alumni and a 34–0 loss to Fostoria. Fremont then went on a tear, rolling off three straight shutout wins before going to Sandusky. Fremont then waxed the Blue and White 42–0. It would stand for more than eighty years as the worst beating Fremont put on its oldest rival. Edbun Eesley and team captain William "Bunk" Ross, the late superintendent's nephew, each scored twice for Fremont, while Harold Wendler and Harold

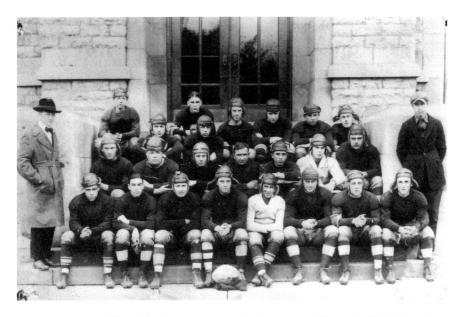

The 1920 Fremont High School team poses on the front steps of Sandusky High School after a 42–0 shutout win over the Blue and White. Fremont would go on to win its second straight Little Big Six title.

Boyer each scored once. Fremont fans were on pins and needles, the *Daily News* reported, not for fear of a loss but for fear of losing their shutout streak.

"The contest was so one-sided that half the crowd was watching the sea gulls hover over the city of fish while the other half was thinking about the five votes that Napoleon Bonaparte received in a west end precinct during the late, deceased election," wrote the *Daily Messenger*, under a headline saying that Sandusky was "buried under an avalanche of points."

Fremont finished the season with seven straight wins to claim its second consecutive league title. After being blanked in two losses to begin the season, all of Fremont's wins came by shutout. The *Daily Messenger* would refer to the 1920 team as the "champions of all champions."

By 1921, the Little Big Six had become the Little Big Seven, with the addition of Oberlin. Expectations were high for Fremont. "Indications point to one of the greatest teams that every represented Fremont High," wrote Colonel James O'Farrell in the *Messenger*. Fremont began the season with two straight wins—a non-league game at Lima Central, and a league contest at home with Norwalk. But Fremont was put on its heels with losses at home to new member Oberlin and a one-point heartbreaker at Lorain. The loss to Lorain gave the Steelmen the conference lead but also put Sandusky in the driver's seat. If it could beat Lorain, it would have a clear path to the league title.

The Lorain game turned out to be the last game of the season for Fremont, which had postponed games against Sandusky and Huron because of a smallpox outbreak in the city. Two boys had attended the junior high school with the disease, during its two-week incubation period, exposing their classmates to smallpox. Soon, the disease was rampant throughout the city, causing the county health department to ban any public gatherings and close the schools. Sandusky and Oberlin shared the Little Big Seven title that year.

Charles Taylor, a former Ohio State football player, became the Fremont football coach in 1922, and the *Messenger* said his presence could make Fremont a dark horse candidate for the league title. Sandusky was concerned enough to send scouts to practice, according to the *Messenger*, and Fremont was 2–1 going into the matchup. As it turned out, Sandusky needn't have worried. The Blue and White pasted their rivals 32–0, with scores by Borders, Walton, Shepherd and Krebs (two). It was the first game at the new high school field in Sandusky.

The Sandusky loss sent Fremont into a spiral. It didn't win another game that year, and it dropped the first two games of 1923, to Elyria and Lorain. Taylor brought his former Ohio State teammate, Pete Stinchcomb of Fostoria, to practice with Fremont to try to get the team to perform to its potential.

"They are big, rangy, game and have been drilled well and know the rudiments of the grand old turf scramble," O'Farrell wrote. "But there's something missing."

Fremont managed a couple ties, against Norwalk and Fostoria, before losing to Bellevue and at Bowling Green to go into the Sandusky game 0–4–2. Julius "Judy" Lerch scored twice for Fremont, which prevailed 13–6. Shepherd scored for Sandusky in the loss.

"The football motor is now whirring along the main road instead of being hampered by a lot of muddy detours and impaired roads," O'Farrell wrote.

O'Farrell was so ecstatic about the win (and since it was a Saturday game and the *Messenger* didn't print until Monday, he wasn't on deadline) that he composed a poem celebrating the win:

> *There was Hurley, Thatcher, Nickles and Zink,*
> *Who whipsawed 'em cockeyed and made 'em see pink.*
> *Came Danny Reardon, Siler, Hawk and "Sly" Fox*
> *Knockin' 'em cuckoo and out of their sox.*

Witness Hughes, "Coy" Gusty, Engler and Lerch,
Making 'em warble and sing from a perch.
Add Taylor, Bloom, Schneider and the rest of the pack,
And you'll have that game gang that staged a comeback.

Fremont won its next two games to finish 3–4–2, while Sandusky finished 3–8.

The Purple and White were a little cocky going into the 1924 Sandusky game, at least according to newspaper reports. The *Messenger* reported that Fremont expected to win by at least three touchdowns and quoted a fan as saying that the only team better in northwest Ohio was Toledo Waite, which at that point was on its way to a national high school title. "If they get whipped, there will be no excuses to offer," Colonel O'Farrell wrote of Fremont. "But they aren't going to get whipped."

Instead, the teams played to a stalemate. Kenny Hawk ran for what appeared to be a forty-yard touchdown, but he was ruled out of bounds at the four-yard line. The Sandusky defense held, and the teams battled to a scoreless tie. "The Purple and White battled the Blue and White until black and blue predominated," a chastened O'Farrell wrote.

The tie didn't hurt Fremont's league standing, but it didn't help either. If the Purple and White won the following week in the season finale against Oberlin, they would clinch the runner-up spot in the Little Big Seven. But Oberlin prevailed handily, 30–7, and Fremont settled for third with a 3–2–1 league record—one spot above Sandusky, which finished with a 2–2–2 record. Fremont finished 5–3–1 overall, while Sandusky finished 3–4–3.

In 1925, an undersized Fremont team beat Sandusky 8–6 in the last Fremont High School football game at the Sandusky County Fairgrounds. "The story can be written in two words," wrote the *Fremont Daily Messenger*. "Kenny Hawk." Hawk, a sophomore, ran twenty-seven times for 237 yards, including the game-winning touchdown, a 25-yard scamper that was downplayed by the *Sandusky Star Journal*.

"Hawk's run wasn't so sensational, and it was made possible through Sandusky poor tackling," the *Star Journal* wrote in a case of sour grapes. Hawk was the leading scorer for Fremont that year, with four touchdowns. Today, there are players who score more in a single game, but Hawk accounted for all but one of Fremont's touchdowns that season. Hawk would transfer to Toledo Waite the following season.

Billy Nicholson caught a touchdown pass to put Sandusky on the board against Fremont, and Vic Weis fumbled for the Blue and White at Sandusky's three-yard line. Although he recovered the ball, he was tackled in the end zone for Fremont's first points of the game.

At that point, the Fremont team was referred to as the Yellow Devils, because of their yellow headgear, or Purple and White, because of the school colors. The *Daily Messenger* referred to them previously as the Big Red or the Zebras, for their purple-and-white-striped jerseys. Monte Glatz, sports editor of the *Fremont Daily News*, wrote, "Fremont can be proud of its 'Little Giants,' who outclassed the team that defeated Norwalk and held Lorain and Elyria to low scores." Several years later, the crosstown *Messenger* started calling them the Bob Cats, saying they'd outgrown the Little Giants nickname—a charge mocked by the *Daily News*.

"Change the name of the 'Little Giants' after all these years? Not by a jugful we won't. The 'Little Giants' were born in the mud and water of that titan struggle with Sandusky in 1925 and 'Little Giants' they'll stay as far as this department was concerned," the *News* wrote.

Ultimately, Little Giants won out, and by 1938, the *Daily News* and *Messenger* merged to form the *News-Messenger*, which continues to this day.

Sandusky ended the 1925 season with a visit from Findlay High School on Thanksgiving. The "Golden Tornado" put on a clinic, beating Sandusky 32–0 before the biggest crowd in school history. Accounts of the day said that paid attendance was 3,054, but complimentary admissions and gatecrashers brought the actual total to around 3,200. Fremont had also hoped for a Turkey Day high school football game, and plans were discussed for a matchup between Fremont and Gibsonburg to settle the Sandusky County championship, but it couldn't be scheduled. Fremont football fans were treated to a game at the fairgrounds between the Fremont Merchants All-Stars, a team of local high school alumni who had played in college or on various semi-pro teams, and the Sandusky Maroons, one of the semi-pro teams that dotted the football landscape. (Maroons was a popular name for football teams of the era. The Toledo NFL entry was the Maroons, as was a team in Pottsville, Pennsylvania, which has gained mythical status for its 1925 NFL title that was taken away by the league). Local restaurants offered special holiday hours for people to eat and watch football. A crowd of more than 2,000 people gathered for the game.

The following year, the biggest rivalry game of the year for both teams would become a part of Thanksgiving.

CHAPTER 3

THANKSGIVING MATCHUPS

With no need to worry about playoff starts, it wasn't uncommon for the high school football season in Ohio to stretch through November, with rivalry games played on Thanksgiving.

Piqua and Troy met on Thanksgiving, as did South and Rayen in Youngstown and Waite and Scott in Toledo. The American Professional Football Association played a full schedule of Thanksgiving games in 1920, its inaugural year, and continued to schedule Thanksgiving games throughout the 1920s as it became the National Football League.

In 1926, Fremont High School and Sandusky met for the first time on Thanksgiving, battling to a 0–0 tie at High School Field in Sandusky. Bunk Ross, the captain of the 1920 Little Big Six champion Fremont team, had succeeded Taylor as coach.

"Six times during that game, the Blue and White machine drove deep into Fremont's territory, and six times did Fremont rise to the occasion and repulse the attack," said an account in the 1928 program for the annual game, taken from the *Sandusky Register*. Karl Krueger attempted two field goals, but both times the ball struck the crossbar of the goal post, leaving a muddy mark as "mute evidence of Sandusky's near-victory" before a crowd estimated at 3,500. The Little Giants also had two field goals bounce off the goal posts.

Ross resigned as coach after the 1926 season, but the school couldn't find a replacement, so he returned for two more years.

In 1927, the Little Giants and Sandusky met for the first time at Harmon Field, the new home for Fremont High School football. More than six

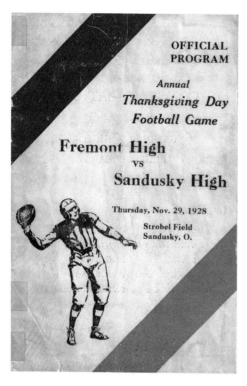

OFFICIAL
PROGRAM

Annual
Thanksgiving Day
Football Game

Fremont High
vs
Sandusky High

Thursday, Nov. 29, 1928

Strobel Field
Sandusky, O.

Cover from the 1928 Thanksgiving Day game program.

thousand people crammed into the field, a league record. A Fremont win would garner a share of the Little Big Seven. Sandusky's Johnny Mott tackled Fremont quarterback Harold Althoff in the end zone for a safety, the only points scored during the 2–0 Sandusky win that clinched a Little Big Seven title in Ken Mills's first year as coach. The previous five league titles had been won by Lorain, but the team, along with Elyria, left the Little Big Seven for the 1927 season. Tiffin Columbian and Willard joined the league to keep its name accurate.

In 1928, Sandusky won its second straight Little Big Seven conference title with a 3–2 Thanksgiving win over Fremont in front of six thousand fans in Sandusky. In three years, Sandusky had scored a total of five points against Ross and had a 2–0–1 record to show for it. Karl Krueger booted a field goal from the twenty-five-yard line for Sandusky. A potential touchdown pass by Ross's Harold Althoff went through Les Binkley's fingertips, and Sandusky's Johnny Bettridge deliberately took a late safety to preserve the win, which gave the Blue Streaks their first undefeated season in modern school history, as the team went 8–0–1. The tie game was against high school power Toledo Waite, giving Sandusky credibility as a team.

In 1929, a replacement for Bunk Ross was finally found, as Robert Oldfather took over as Fremont coach. Fans got to watch the 1929 Thanksgiving Day game in a blinding snowstorm—the only snow of that winter, in fact. Sandusky had clinched the league the game before but was still playing a rivalry game. Edgar Newton, nicknamed "Fig" by Glatz at the *Daily News*, kicked off for Fremont. Newton, who went on to become a local Little League umpire in the Sandusky area, told the *Register* later, "When I kicked the ball, it was gone, and we had no idea who made the grab." He said he then saw a "ghost-like streak through the snow." It was Bettridge, returning the ball eighty-three yards for a touchdown. Bettridge would also score on a forty-three-yard touchdown run. London Gant accounted for both extra points for Sandusky. J.W. Miller scored a touchdown and added an extra point, and Fremont was able to tackle Bettridge in the end zone for a safety to pull within five points. The Little Giants blocked a Sandusky punt, but Bettridge saved the game with a tackle five yards shy of the goal line, and the Sandusky defense held to preserve the 14–9 win.

The 1930 game was once again for the Little Big Seven title. More than five thousand fans braved temperatures that dropped to -3 degrees. John Weis ran for a touchdown in the second quarter for Sandusky, and the Blue Streaks held a 6–0 lead until the fourth, when an Ed Brehm pass to Bob Redding tied the game. The extra-point pass was batted down by Red Harple, and both defenses held. The game ended in a 6–6 tie, and Fremont and Sandusky shared the league title. It was the first of many league titles Sandusky would win under Bob Whittaker, in his first year as Blue Streaks coach. By then, Fremont High School had been renamed in memory of its long-serving superintendent, W.W. Ross.

Sandusky had won each of its first ten games of the 1931 season going into the Thanksgiving Day matchup, but Ross got on the board first with a George Demmel touchdown. "You could even hear their watches tick, it was that still on their side of the field," the *Messenger* wrote. But the Blue Streaks exploded for twenty points in the second quarter, with an offensive touchdown by Weis to tie the game and a touchdown pass by London Gant to Harple to put Sandusky in the lead. Weis then had a thirty-eight-yard pick-six, running "like a Chinaman leaving Manchuria," according to the *Messenger*, to give Sandusky a 20–6 halftime lead. Gant would run for a score, and Pete Peterson would add a touchdown for Ross in a 26–12 Sandusky win that clinched the fifth straight league title for the Blue and White.

The following year, there would be no league title at stake when Ross met Sandusky. The Blue Streaks and Little Giants each had two losses. The Little Giants, as reported in the next day's *Messenger*, folded "like a collapsible porch chair" and "went into complete hibernation," as Sandusky had its way in a 33–0 win. Burns ran for a pair of touchdowns, and Gant threw for two scores and caught another touchdown pass. Gant, a senior who ended his high school career with sixty touchdowns, was described as "three-fifths pile driver and two-fifths kangaroo." He was so fearsome that schools didn't believe he was really seventeen, and a doctor at Western Reserve University in Cleveland offered to X-ray Gant's bones to determine his age. There is no indication he was taken up on his offer.

In 1933, the Blue Streaks went undefeated again, culminating in an 18–0 win over Ross. All the points in the game were scored in the first quarter, as Gene Burns, described in the *Toledo News-Bee* as the "Sandusky Negro backfield ace," returned a punt ninety-five yards to score. Al Hess scored twice, on runs of sixty-nine and fifty-eight yards, as the Blue Streaks "rolled over a game but outclassed band of gridders," according to the *News-Bee*, to an 18-0 win. The win enabled the Blue Streaks to finish 11–0 and "tighten their claims on the mythical scholastic championship of Ohio," the paper reported.

After that season, the Little Big Seven went down to the Little Big Five with the departure of Fremont, Sandusky and Tiffin and the addition of Port Clinton. It went down to four two years later with the departure of Oberlin before fading away in 1944.

Ross, Sandusky and Tiffin formed a new league with Findlay and Fostoria called the Buckeye League. The remnants of the Little Big Seven—Bellevue, Norwalk and Willard—would form the Northern Ohio League with Bucyrus, Crestline, Galion, Shelby and Upper Sandusky, while Port Clinton left.

In the twenty-one years Ross spent in the Little Big Seven, it had won just two league titles outright, in 1919 and 1920, and shared the 1930 title with the Blue Streaks, the nickname coined by *Sandusky Star-Journal* sportswriter Len Winkler, who would spend thirty years as the voice of Sandusky High School athletics. Sandusky dominated the league during its existence, winning or sharing ten titles, including six of the last seven. The Blue Streaks forfeited four games in 1915 to cost them another league title.

Ross and Sandusky met on Thanksgiving 1934 with a new league title at stake. The Blue Streaks were 3–0 in the Buckeye League, while Ross was 2–0–1. Among the thousands of attendees was Johnny Bettridge, the former Sandusky star playing at Ohio State. Bettridge, who would go on to have a brief professional career with the Chicago Bears and Cleveland Rams, watched from the press box at Strobel Field. Haldon Binkley accounted for all of Ross's scoring, with a touchdown and a field goal, and the Little Giants actually took a 9–0 lead into halftime. "Coach Bob Whittaker must have taken Lincoln's Gettysburg speech all apart when he tongue-lashed his charges in the between-the-halves session," wrote the *Messenger*.

It worked, as Don Whittaker (Bob's brother) and Bob Schillig scored touchdowns to put Sandusky ahead. Ross drove down to the five-inch line but couldn't score, as time ran out on a 13–9 Sandusky win.

Earlier that year, the Portsmouth Spartans, which two years earlier had played in the first NFL playoff game, losing to the Chicago Bears, were bought by a syndicate headed by George Richards of Detroit. Richards, the owner of WJR, moved the team to the Motor City and renamed it the Lions. The namesake was the king of the jungle, Richards said, and the team would soon be the king of the NFL. That year, the Lions played one of three games on Thanksgiving and, except for World War II, has hosted its own Turkey Day game ever since.

The Blue Streaks were riding a thirty-three-game win streak into the 1935 Thanksgiving matchup against Ross. Sandusky had gone undefeated in 1933 and 1934, and although the game was against two undefeated teams, the Blue Streaks were installed as twenty-one-point favorites, according to the *Daily Messenger*. More than 5,500 advance tickets were sold, and total attendance numbered around 8,000.

Sandusky got out to a 13–0 halftime lead with two touchdowns by LaMar Krueger. A pass interference call put Ross on the Sandusky five-yard line in the fourth quarter, and three plays later, LeRoy Littler punched it in from a yard out. The extra point made it 13–7, the final score.

Lee Faris demonstrated in that Friday's *Daily Messenger* that stat-keeping was more of an art than a science. Fremont statisticians said the Little Giants outgained Sandusky 137–119, but Sandusky number crunchers gave the Blue Streaks the edge, 150–130.

The Little Giants' seven points were the most scored on Sandusky in a game that year. The Blue Streaks went 11–0, outscoring their opponents 455–19 and pitching eight shutouts. Not only did Sandusky win the league crown; it could also lay claim to a mythical state title. But there was a new team in ascent in northeast Ohio, and its success and reputation would bedevil Sandusky and Ross for years to come.

After a 1–9 season in 1931, Massillon High School went looking for a new coach. It found alumnus and former Miami football player Paul Brown. A Norwalk native, Brown took the job and within two years had turned the Tigers into a high school football powerhouse—coinciding with the Blue Streaks' dominance on the opposite end of the state. So while Sandusky could make a case for a state title, Massillon was proclaimed it—and won the National Sports News Service national title that year as well, the first of four that Brown would win before going on to bigger and better things.

Once again, in 1936, the league title would come down to the Ross-Sandusky game. The Blue Streaks' winning streak rolled up to thirty-seven games before a 14–7 loss to Toledo Waite, four years removed from its second

NSNS national title. Ross, meanwhile, was 7–1–1. And once again, Sandusky went off to an early 13–0 lead, starting with a touchdown pass by Albert Ohlemacher to Harold Krause in the first quarter. In the third, Krause blew through the Ross defensive line for a twenty-six-yard touchdown run. Ross scored late on a fifteen-yard touchdown strike by Pete Fox to Glenn Balsizer. And once again, Sandusky had beaten Ross and won the Buckeye League title. Expected attendance was around 8,000, but because of biting cold and snow, actual attendance was around 5,500.

The 1937 Sandusky football team, which started five sophomores, three juniors and three seniors, was regarded as one of the greenest in recent memory—and lost its first three games out of the gate. Ross, on the other hand, started the season 7–2 under new coach Fred McClintock. Oldfather had taken a job as principal at Napoleon High School and had given up his coaching duties. Both teams were undefeated in the league going into the Thanksgiving Day matchup. To give an idea of the priorities of the day, the banner headline on the front page of the *Messenger* the day before Thanksgiving proclaimed, "7,500 to See Ross Battle Sandusky." A subhead under it said that hundreds would attend a religious service in Fremont. The game was another Sandusky rout, as Al Gant, London's brother, and Geno Balconi each scored two touchdowns in a 26–0 whitewash, the third Sandusky shutout in six meetings and the tenth Blue Streak win in twelve years. The other two games were ties.

There was already talk of Sandusky leaving the Buckeye League. It would maintain its rivalry games with Ross and Tiffin Columbian, but the rest of the league was tired of taking regular beatings from the Blue Streaks, who were the class of football in Ohio. They'd continue to play the league in other sports, but Sandusky would go independent in football—which was pitched as an advantage to the Blue Streaks, who were always a big draw and could play other teams in the region. "Turnstiles always click merrily with local fans regardless of whether the game is at home or away," wrote the *Sandusky Register*, which also pointed out that with paid attendance in Fremont at 6,307, the Ross athletic coffers swelled with $3,700—with only $250 going to Sandusky.

Ross fans were starting to believe that the losing streak wasn't because Ross was being outplayed but because it was being outcoached. Frank "Ding" Buehler, president of the Fremont Down Town Coaches, wrote a letter to the *Daily News* imploring Ross to give up the rivalry. "Let us swallow our pride and discontinue our series with Sandusky," he wrote. "Let us admit they are too good for us."

Edwin Erchenbrecher Sr. of South Street in Fremont responded in another a letter to the editor, reaching back to the city's history to excoriate Buehler and those who wanted to drop Sandusky from the Ross schedule:

> *Did Col. Croghan and his sharpshooters defending the fort on the very hill across from where our beloved Ross High School now stands fear the British Lion and his savage allies when they came from the same lake shore in 1813 to blast us out of the picture (or fort, rather)?*
>
> *No, no, a thousand times no. So why should we, some hundred odd years later, fear to play football with a group of husky young men from the same port? Brave old Col. Croghan would turn over in his grave at such rank cowardice.*

Erchenbrecher advocated hiring better coaches and stacked Ross's athletic talent up with anyone else's.

"If our boys are taught football as early as the Sanduskians, with an adequate coaching group," he wrote, "we should be able, in several years, to compete with them on at least an equal basis."

Erchenbrecher then returned to his comparison with Colonel Croghan to close his letter, saying, "As Col. Croghan held the fort against Gen. Proctor and his red streaks, so let us continue to hold the line against the Sandusky Blue Streaks, for though the old guard may die, it never surrenders."

In 1938, the two teams met for the last time on Thanksgiving. Whittaker had previously suggested playing Ross earlier in the year.

On Halloween of that year, Orson Welles and his Mercury Radio Theater put on a broadcast of "War of the Worlds" that led people to believe—in the finest tradition of radio as theater of the mind—that aliens had really invaded New Jersey. In that spirit, Sandusky student Dave Kroft wrote an article for Ross's *Croghan Chatter* detailing a 36–0 Ross victory—which would have been the first Ross win since 1925.

In real life, Bob Blakely scored for Sandusky in the first. In the second, Al Koebel scored for Ross from a yard out on a play set up by Sandusky being whistled for an illegal substitution—of Blakely, no less. The game remained 7–6 favoring Sandusky going into the fourth, but touchdowns by Al Gant, Ben Fleming and Geno Balconi put the game out of reach, giving Sandusky the 28–7 win to finish the season 8–0–1. The tie came in Week Two against Elyria, a 0–0 scoreless tie—one of eight shutouts pitched by the Streaks defense that year. Sandusky was a yard away from scoring to win that game when time ran out. Ross, meanwhile, finished 3–7.

The Blue Streaks won the Buckeye League crown and promptly left the league. Oscar Ruhl, the sports editor of the *Mansfield News-Journal*, suggested a "superconference" of Sandusky, Mansfield, Canton McKinley, Massillon, Elyria and Lorain. It never happened, but four of those six teams would go on to form the Buckeye Conference.

Jerry Liska, sports editor for the *Fremont News-Messenger* (created that year when the *Daily News* and *Messenger* merged) said it was about time Sandusky left the league, having won the last six titles.

"It is hard to imagine why loop officials permitted the iron fist of the Blue Streaks to pulverize far weaker members for the past four years," wrote Liska, who would go on to serve as the Associated Press sports editor in Chicago and president of the Football Writers of America.

But the end of Sandusky's league membership wouldn't mean the end of its annual meeting with Ross. "When these sparse locks are silver strands," Liska wrote, "Sandusky and Fremont will still be tangling through the fierce pride of two rival cities. They can lick us, but they can't make us quit."

In 1939, the game was played on a Saturday afternoon—Armistice Day (now Veterans Day), November 11. There were efforts to move the game to an evening start, since merchants had no desire to close up shops during a Saturday afternoon after payday, but it ended up remaining an afternoon game. Sandusky went into the game 4–4, including a loss to perpetual power Waite, while Ross was 7–1. There was no league title at stake, but according to Liska, it didn't matter.

"The Buckeye angle always was shunted to the background when these two schools clashed, for the simple reason that the natural rivalry existing between Fremont and Sandusky has overshadowed every other factor," he wrote.

For added drama, Sandusky quarterback Ernie Thomas had been injured in the previous game and was recuperating in a Toledo hospital, prompting the cry of "Win it for Ernie!"

The Little Giants outgained Sandusky 395–257, but Ross also threw three key interceptions as the Blue Streaks won 19–0. Ben Fleming scored on a fake punt for Sandusky in the fourth and also caught a pitch from Lyle Reichert to Bob Shaw, running it sixty yards for another score. Balconi added a touchdown for Sandusky in the fourth. Even with the loss, Ross won the Buckeye League title, its first league title since 1930 and first outright since 1920.

Shaw, who was the leading scorer in the state with nineteen touchdowns going into the game, was held in check, carrying the ball just seven times. He would go on to score five touchdowns in a game against Bowling Green, as Sandusky was no longer the last game of the year for Ross. His 154 points in 1939 are still fourth in Fremont Ross history. Later that month, he, coach Fred McClintock and Liska were guests of Ohio State coach Francis Schmidt for the Buckeyes game against Michigan in Ann Arbor, as Tom Harmon led the Wolverines from a 14–0 deficit to a 21–14 win.

Shaw went on to play for Schmidt—and his successor, Paul Brown, who left Massillon for the Buckeyes coaching job. Shaw was an all-American on the 1942 Ohio State national champion team. After serving in World War II, Shaw played professional football for the Cleveland Rams, where he was regarded as the first tight end; the Chicago Cardinals; and in the Canadian Football League. He also coached in the CFL and NFL and was a charter member of the Ross Hall of Fame, as well as an inductee into the Ohio State Hall of Fame.

Also in 1939, the first postseason high school football game was played in Ohio. The Buckeye Bowl, played at Ohio Stadium in Columbus, was approved by OHSAA commissioner H.R. Townsend, and early indications were that Massillon would play Portsmouth. But Paul Brown expressed no interest in the game, and Portsmouth instead played powerhouse Toledo Waite, which traveled coast to coast to play football teams and won NSNS national titles in 1924 and 1932. It appeared Waite wouldn't play either, as the Toledo Public Schools faced a financial crunch and considered closing the schools from November until after the first of the year, but that situation was resolved, and the Indians handed Portsmouth its first loss in twenty-six games, 9–7, laying claim to the state championship. The Tigers were also named NSNS national champions, further muddying the waters. The following year, the Indians went to new Tiger Stadium in Massillon and proceeded to get thumped 28–0, proving…well, nothing. As long as state and national championships weren't decided on the field, they would always be mythical.

The Buckeye Bowl turned out to be a one-off. Although pre-game crowd estimates ranged from 10,000 to 20,000, only 3,947 showed up, blamed in part on a steady cold rain. Interest in postseason football waned after that. There were talks of a Lorain-Massillon postseason matchup in 1940, but the Lorain High School athletic association opposed it, and superintendent Paul Bunn agreed, stating:

> *I am convinced that school authorities cannot justify the playing of football or any other sport on the grounds that it is a money-making proposition.*

When we commercialize high school football, we defeat the very purpose of playing the game and we are guilty of exploiting the members of the team who play the game for the game's sake and not to make money. When a school has a winning team, there is always the danger in mind that football exists for the school and not the school for football. To use a homely expression, we should never allow "the tail to wag the dog."

Neither Ross nor Sandusky was having a good year going into the 1940 meeting. The Little Giants had one win, while the Blue Streaks had two. But once the game started, it wasn't even a remotely even matchup, as Sandusky handed Ross the worst loss in the rivalry, beating the Little Giants 46–0. Ben Fleming scored four touchdowns for Sandusky and booted three extra points.

"A gory little drama called 'Murder Under the Stars' took place at Strobel Field in Sandusky Friday night, as the Blue Streaks of Sandusky High bludgeoned the Little Giants of Ross High, 46-0, before a shivering throng of 5,000," the *News-Messenger* wrote.

In 1940, Whittaker left Sandusky—much to the relief of fans of Ross and the Blue Streaks' other opponents—to become the head football coach at Bowling Green State University. By then, Sandusky superintendent Frank Prout had gone on to become the university's president.

Under Whittaker, the Streaks outscored their opponents 2,597–637 and only allowed more than 100 points in one season, when they gave up 140 in 1940. Whittaker coached the Falcon football team for fourteen years, compiling a 66–50–7 record as Bowling Green went from the Ohio Athletic Conference to independent to its current home in the Mid-American Conference. However, he went 6–12–1 in the MAC before being replaced by Doyt Perry, a former assistant to Woody Hayes at Ohio State.

Whittaker stayed on as the track coach, a role he had also served in Sandusky. His ten-year tenure as head coach included two undefeated seasons and one MAC runner-up finish. He served an additional five years as an assistant. Perry is the namesake for the football stadium on campus, but the track is named for Whittaker.

Whittaker's biggest point of pride in Sandusky? He never lost to Fremont. The Blue Streaks were 10–0–1 against their rivals to the south between 1930 and 1940, having gone 86–20–2 overall.

"They tied us one year, but that was it," said Whittaker. "Fremont never beat us in my eleven years as coach."

CHAPTER 4

THE RIVALRY'S HOMES

STROBEL FIELD AND HARMON FIELD

In the early years of the rivalry (which coincided with the infancy of football), the home teams bounced around. Both schools were in county seats, so both teams made liberal use of their county fairgrounds. Fremont played at the County Fairgrounds as well as Wasserman, Lipstraw and Herbrand Parks. Sandusky's home fields included the baseball park at the corner of Columbus and Perkins Avenues and various fairground sites.

In 1921, the Sandusky School Board bought a plot of land for a new athletic complex, which was dedicated in 1922 prior to the Fremont game. The 1923 Fram, the Sandusky annual, called it "a beautiful athletic field which ranks among the best in the state," which included a football field, a grandstand and a track that was attractive enough to the OHSAA to schedule sectional meets there.

In 1936, on the same site, a new steel-and-concrete stadium was built. Strobel Field was named for longtime school board member C.J. Strobel. The project, built by the federal Works Progress Administration, a public works program set up by President Franklin Roosevelt, was estimated to cost around $100,000. It included a new track, locker and training rooms, a spacious press box (including broadcast booths) and lights so games could be played at night. That was visionary, as Major League Baseball was still two years away from its first night game.

More than eight thousand people came out for the dedication ceremony on September 25, 1936, preceding the game against Elyria. The Blue

Strobel Field, Sandusky

To the right, today's battle ground—Strobel Field, stamping ground of the Blue Streaks of Sandusky High. The picture shows only the football gridiron, club house and permanent west bleachers. To the east of the football facilities, the field includes quarter mile running track, straightaways and space for baseball diamond. This property was purchased and developed by the Sandusky board of education and first used in 1922. The permanent bleachers on the west side of the gridiron seat nearly 3,000 persons. The field, known as High School Field until 1927, is now named after C. J. Strobel, assistant cashier of the Citizens' Banking Co. and for more than 30 years a member of the Sandusky board of education.

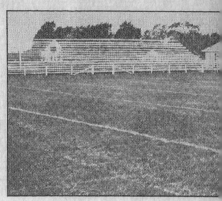

The 1928 Fremont-Sandusky program showed photos of the home fields for both teams.

Streaks prevailed 16–7 for their thirty-sixth straight win. Roy Gant and Harold Krause scored for Sandusky.

Meanwhile, in Fremont, William E. Harmon donated $21,000 to the Fremont Board of Education in 1925. Harmon, an Ohio native, had grown up in the Oklahoma territory, living under constant threat of Indian attack. He was determined to ensure good recreation facilities and donated far and wide to establish athletic fields (home fields in Wapakoneta and Miamisburg, among other places, are also Harmon Field). He also donated land in Lebanon, Ohio, for a golf course.

Wooden bleachers were set up on the land, as was a stone with a plaque commemorating Harmon that reads, "This playfield was made ours through the assistance of the Harmon Foundation. Dedicated forever

Harmon Field, Fremont

The picture to the left, by Frank B. Finch, Fremont, shows Harmon Field, home of Fremont High's football elevens, and the crowd of about 6,000 persons which gathered there Thanksgiving Day, 1927, to witness the Sandusky-Fremont Highs' annual game. It was, up to that date, the largest throng which had ever witnessed a Little Big Seven athletic event. The field, which includes a gridiron, running track and ample bleachers, also has a field house. It takes its name from the Harmon Foundation which provided a substantial fund toward establishment of the field.

to the plays of children, the development of youth and recreation of all. 'The gift of land is a gift eternal.'" Fremont opened the stadium with a 0–0 tie against Bradner.

In 1935, Harmon Field got a seventy-two-thousand-watt floodlighting system to allow for night games to be played there. The Little Giants' first night game was held on September 20, 1935, a 57–0 drubbing of Genoa, the most points scored by a Ross team since 1929. With football practice now starting in July and the season starting in August, it's hard to imagine, but the September 20 game was the season opener for Ross.

The season ended with the Thanksgiving game against Sandusky, a 13–7 loss. The next day, the press box and bleachers were torn down—not by fans rioting because of Ross being unable to beat Sandusky since 1925, but by a Works Progress Administration crew. The Little Giants would play in a new $55,000 concrete-and-steel stadium.

The grandstand at Strobel Field, shortly after its completion in 1937. *Photo courtesy Sandusky Library.*

Throughout Ohio—and the nation—stadiums were springing up as part of public works projects from the New Deal. In addition to Harmon Field in Fremont and Strobel Field in Sandusky, Fawcett Stadium in Canton and Tiger Stadium in Massillon were built by the WPA.

The Little Giants christened their new stadium on October 16, 1936, against Tiffin Columbian. Fans were taken inside the huddle for the opening coin toss, as microphones were placed on the field so people in the stands could listen in. The Little Giants prevailed 26–0.

The Ross-Sandusky game in 1951 at Harmon Field was marred by the collapse of wooden visitors bleachers. No serious injuries were reported, but plans were made to replace them with new metal bleachers.

In 1955, the Sandusky School Board bought a plot of land at the corner of Hayes and Perkins Avenues—almost directly across the street from Strobel Field—for a new high school. An Ohio State study recommended placing the new high school near the field. Also that year, Fremont voters approved a $2.9 million bond issue for a high school on North Street, a block away from Harmon Field.

The new Sandusky High School, built at a cost of $3.66 million, was dedicated and opened in 1957. A year after that, the high school on Croghan Street in Fremont became the junior high school, and Fremont Ross High School opened, serving students in grades ten through twelve.

A postcard of Strobel Field. *Photo courtesy Sandusky Library.*

An aerial view of Harmon Field in the 1980s. The track had been moved to its current location behind the high school. *Photo courtesy Fremont City Schools.*

By the dawn of the twenty-first century, both stadiums were starting to show their age. Visiting teams refused to use the showers at Harmon Field—which had been derided as early as the mid-1950s—and the visitors' bleachers at Strobel were mocked as worthy of condemnation.

In 1998, the Fremont Area Athletic Foundation was formed to raise funds to improve athletic facilities throughout the school system. New baseball and softball fields were built behind Ross High School; a new pool, wrestling room and classrooms were added to the high school; and plans were made for a new stadium on the same site.

The Houston Astrodome, billed as the eighth wonder of the world, was the first fully enclosed stadium when it opened in 1965. But it couldn't sustain a grass field, so artificial turf—called Astroturf—was invented. It wasn't comfortable and could cause injuries, like turf toe. But by the 2000s, it had been supplanted by a new generation of artificial turf, offering a feel similar to that of real grass.

Thanks to a donation by local auto dealer Don Paul, FieldTurf was installed at Harmon Field (now renamed Don Paul Stadium at Harmon Field) for the 2005 season. At that point, a high school playing surface of FieldTurf was a novelty in northwest Ohio, with Frost-Kalnow Stadium in

Tiffin (which was home to college football teams as well) being the only other stadium with an artificial surface.

The Little Giants lost every game in the initial season on the turf (but won every road game that year). After the season was over, the old grandstand was razed, and construction started on a new home grandstand that would offer better sight lines and better facilities for players and coaches from Ross, St. Joseph Central Catholic and any visiting teams during the regular season or playoffs.

The 2006 football season opened with a gleaming new brick-and-aluminum grandstand, and the Little Giants christened it with a 62–14 win over Perrysburg, as Ross went on to go undefeated and host a playoff game for the first time since 1983.

By the time the Greater Buckeye Conference broke up in 2011, the only schools in the league without turf were Napoleon and Sandusky—and the Blue Streaks were installing it. The turf in Sandusky also led to a name change to Strobel Field at Cedar Point Stadium, thanks to a $500,000 donation from the amusement park. Turf had become more commonplace. Ross was joining the Three Rivers Athletic Conference, which had new stadiums at St. John's Jesuit and Toledo Central Catholic, both with turf fields, in addition to Findlay and Lima Senior, old GBC rivals that also had turf. Locally, Clyde and Huron in the Sandusky Bay Conference also played on turf.

And although artificial turf was not a requirement to host neutral site playoff games, it was preferred, making Sandusky and Fremont—both good locations with ample parking and easily accessible from highways and the Ohio Turnpike—even more attractive to the OHSAA.

CHAPTER 5

MAL, BIG THUNDER AND LITTLE THUNDER

ROSS RULES THE RIVALRY IN THE 1950S

For the first time in thirteen years, a Ross alumnus was football coach at his alma mater in 1941. Fred McClintock had given way to Lester Binkley, a 1929 graduate who had played for Bunk Ross—the last Ross graduate to coach the Little Giants—and was part of the 1928 basketball team that advanced to the state tournament. Binkley, who at six feet, four inches tall was nicknamed "Legs," went to Miami of Ohio for a year but spent most of his collegiate career at Western State Teachers College in Kalamazoo, Michigan (now Western Michigan University). He served as an assistant football coach at Detroit River Rouge High School before returning to Fremont in 1938 as one of McClintock's assistants.

Sandusky also had a new coach that year, as Wallace Glenright replaced Bob Whittaker after his departure for Bowling Green State University. The rivalry game had moved to the middle of the season, with Ross sporting a 3–1 record going into the game. The Blue Streaks, meanwhile, were winless in four games. Ed Fox scored two touchdowns (one on an interception return) as the Little Giants finally got the Sandusky monkey off their backs with a 14–7 win. It was the first time Fremont had beaten Sandusky since 1925 (the two teams had tied twice in the interim). Bob Cooper scored a touchdown for Sandusky, which got down inside Ross's four-yard line late in the fourth quarter but was unable to punch it in.

Ross was 3–1 going into the matchup in 1942, while Sandusky was 1–3, but the *News-Messenger* deemed the game a toss-up, as the Blue Streaks had played a tougher schedule. Sandusky prevailed 15–7 on a rainy Strobel Field. Bob Cooper and Dick Marshall scored for the Blue Streaks, and Ross's Jim Wisbon fumbled the ball on the Ross ten-yard line and was tackled in the end zone after he dove on it for a Sandusky safety. The Little Giants got on the board in the fourth quarter with Howard Tiefke's only touchdown of the season.

By then, the United States was in the thick of World War II. The Arsenal of Democracy was mobilizing, and both towns were participating in scrap metal drives, growing victory gardens and making sacrifices in their meals for the war effort. The week of the Ross-Sandusky game, headlines in local newspapers told of U.S. Marines holding Guadalcanal in the South Pacific and the German Army waging war against the Russians in Stalingrad. Where there would be a line in the paper separating stories, there were four words: "Buy War Savings Bonds."

Ross and Sandusky didn't meet in 1943, as Sandusky superintendent Karl Whinnery suspended all sports because of the war. It was the first time the two teams hadn't met on the football field since 1921, when Fremont played a shortened season because of a smallpox outbreak.

Many men from Ross and Sandusky were serving their country at that time. Lenny Thom, a 1935 Sandusky graduate who played football for Francis Schmidt at Ohio State, served on a patrol torpedo boat in the South Pacific commanded by a future president. Thom was on the deck when *PT-109*, commanded by a Harvard graduate named John F. Kennedy, was struck and cut in half by a Japanese destroyer. Thom lived through the adventure and was awarded the Navy and Marine Corps Medal. He later commanded his own PT boat before returning to Ohio, where he was killed when his car struck a train at a blind railroad crossing near Ravenna in 1946.

In 1944, Binkley traded in his coaching whistle for a sailor's hat, joining the U.S. Navy. He was succeeded as coach by Sylvester "Sive" Kohr. Sandusky was back on the schedule, and the two teams battled to a 0–0 tie. Ross had two touchdowns called back for penalties in what turned out to be the only game that year in which the Little Giants were unable to score. Ross went 8–1–1 to win the Buckeye League.

Also in 1944, the Hearst International News Service started ranking high school football teams, putting an end to the era in which high school football teams could proclaim themselves to be state champions. At the end of the year, the wire services, which were already in the practice of naming all-state football teams, would award a poll championship to the top vote getter. No longer would schools be able to declare themselves the state champions.

It was a step in the right direction, but only one team could be crowned state champion in each poll, without any allowance for school size. Wire services had started using polls eleven years earlier for college football, which occupied a lot of attention in the world of sports—certainly more so than the professional game.

In 1945, Ross and Sandusky were each 3–1 going into the matchup, but Sandusky prevailed 14–0, with two touchdowns by Fulton Graves. The *News-Messenger* made it sound like the game wasn't even that close, with the Blue Streaks outgaining the Little Giants 290 yards to 57 and earning sixteen first downs compared with Ross's three. At the end of the year, Ross fans got to share in the glory of Bob Shaw, who helped the Cleveland Rams win the NFL title with a 15–14 win over the Washington Redskins at Cleveland Stadium. It was the last game the Rams would play as a home team in Cleveland.

Dan Reeves, who had bought the team four years earlier, relocated the team to Los Angeles, as Arch Ward, the *Chicago Tribune* sports editor that brought about the Major League Baseball All-Star Game, was starting a new football league. Professional football teams and leagues had come into being and quickly disappeared, and the NFL itself wasn't always the most financially healthy endeavor either. But the All-American Football Conference quickly took hold in Cleveland, as new owner Mickey McBride, who had become a football fan watching Notre Dame with his son, hired one of the biggest names in football: former Massillon High School and Ohio State football coach Paul Brown. The team, called the Browns, would begin play in 1946 and almost instantly own the league.

Meanwhile, in Fremont, Legs Binkley was back at the helm of the Little Giants in 1946. His opposite number at Sandusky was former Blue Streak Johnny Weis. The Blue Streaks found themselves on the short end of all four games going into the Ross game. They had scored a total of six points and had lost three of the games by at least thirty-nine points. Ross, on the other hand, had shot out of the gate with four straight wins and continued unimpeded with a 19–0 win at Strobel Field. It was the first win for Ross at Strobel, and its first win in Sandusky since the 1920 shutout. Tex Frey scored on an eighty-three-yard run off tackle, and Bob Beck and Dale Hoy also added touchdowns for Ross. Sam Sims spent as much time in the Sandusky backfield as the Blue Streaks' backs, and in a statement that demonstrated how far sports medicine has progressed, the *News-Messenger* reported, "Tom LaRose, Sandusky fullback, was knocked out five times during the course of the game…but nothing serious."

Ross ended the season on a three-game losing streak, but its 6–3 record was good enough to win the Buckeye League for the second time in three years. Binkley would never again coach a Ross team that wasn't Buckeye League champions. Sandusky, meanwhile, went 1–8 and replaced Weis with Vic Malinovsky.

In 1947, Binkley made a great hire, adding former Tiffin Columbian coach Bob Seele as an assistant. The Blue Streaks continued to list, losing their first four games going into the Ross game, and once again had scored just six points. Ross, which was undefeated, won 13–0, but the *News-Messenger* described it as the Little Giants' worst win of the season and "unimpressive." John Auxter and Walter Weinhardt scored for Ross, which gained 235 yards on the ground simply by brute strength, the *News-Messenger* reported. Overall, Ross outgained Sandusky 320–66 and got fifteen first downs to the Blue Streaks' four.

The 1947 Little Giants rose to second in the INS poll before suffering their only loss of the year, to Elyria. That year, the Associated Press also started a high school football poll. Ross went 9–1 to win another Buckeye League title and finished fourteenth in the inaugural Associated Press poll. Sandusky went winless that year, finishing 0–8–1.

Under new coach Jeff DeHaven, Sandusky snapped a twelve-game losing streak the week before the 1948 Ross game with a 33–6 win over Ashland. Ross once again was undefeated going into the rivalry game and won handily, 20–7. Bob Beck scored two touchdowns and two extra points, and Charlie "Twinkletoes" Glover scored a touchdown that was set up by a Dick Sherman fumble recovery. Lavern Ward scored late for Sandusky.

Once again, a potential undefeated season for Ross was undone by Elyria, which beat the Little Giants 13–7. It was the third year in a row that Elyria had beaten Ross, and the second year in a row it handed the Little Giants their first loss of the year. Ross tied Springfield the following week and recovered to beat Marion Harding 13–0 in the season finale to win the Buckeye League for the third straight year.

Expectations were high for the Little Giants in 1949. "All over Northwest Ohio, coaches, fans and newspapers have rated the Giants as the No. 1 team on paper," wrote *News-Messenger* sports editor Al Coxon. Ross rose to sixth in the Associated Press poll going into the game against unbeaten Findlay. The Trojans were ranked fourteenth. But Charlie Glover was out with an ankle injury, and Coxon described the pessimism around Ross as palpable. Findlay won the game 26–13, dropping Ross to fourteenth in the AP poll.

The Little Giants would have to regroup against Sandusky, which was undefeated and ranked tenth in the poll. Blue Streak football appeared to be back, and the *Sandusky Register* reported that talk around town was that Ross was the only obstacle to an unbeaten season for the Blue Streaks.

Bob Markley got Ross on the board, but Ted Schwanger scored for Sandusky to make it 7–6. It was the last time the Blue Streaks would lead. Glover returned and scored two touchdowns, and Markley added another score. But Binkley put two sophomores, both of whom had grown up on Bidwell Avenue in Fremont, into the lineup for their first varsity action, and they made the most of it. John Lewis scored two touchdowns for Ross, and Jerome Surratt would score another in a 47–7 rout. The teammates and friends, who ran track together in the spring and had played sandlot football and baseball growing up, would become two of the most celebrated players in Ross history.

Ross moved up to eighth in the next AP poll, while Sandusky dropped out. The following week, against Tiffin Columbian, John Lewis, in his second varsity start, tied the school record with six touchdowns in a game in a 78–0 rout. More than sixty years later, Lewis is willing to share credit with the offensive line. "That wasn't all me," he said. "We had a hell of a line. Running wasn't that difficult. They opened those holes."

The Little Giants got over their Elyria hex with a 7–0 win, finishing the season 9–1 and ranked fifth in the AP and INS polls. It was the fourth straight year that Ross had won the Buckeye League. Sandusky finished 5–3–1 for its first winning season since 1945.

Binkley's star would never be higher, and the following July, he left Ross for Toledo Waite, still regarded as a state power and a potential steppingstone to a collegiate coaching career. Binkley's departure threw the program into disarray, as it came less than two months before the football season would start. His assistant, Bob Seele, had no interest in the job, but many other coaches did, including some from as far away as Florida and Iowa. Al Coxon pointed out that most of the applicants were from outside the area and drew the conclusion that many area coaches wanted nothing to do with the high-pressure job. The Little Giants had won six of the previous eight Buckeye League titles, and Binkley had gone 48–18–2 as Ross coach, including a 26–3–1 record in the previous three years.

Among the applicants was Malcolm Mackey, a Purdue graduate whose career included a stint as an assistant coach at Western Reserve University (now Case Western Reserve University) in Cleveland. Mackey, whose brother Guy was the athletic director at Purdue (and would serve as the namesake for the school's basketball arena), came highly recommended from his alma mater. Among those endorsing him was Boilermakers assistant coach Jack Mollenkopf, who had spent twelve years as Waite head coach. (Mollenkopf had been on the short list to become Ohio State's coach before the Buckeyes hired Wes Fesler in 1947 and would go on to become the Boilermakers coach—and the namesake for Waite's stadium).

Mackey, a native of New Albany, Indiana, had won two Indiana state titles and was hired by the Fremont school board. He would serve as football and track coach and an assistant basketball coach. (In 1952, he also started the school's wrestling program, and today the Ross home wrestling invitational is named for him). He took the job for $4,050 a year (likely one of his selling points) and was certified to teach social studies, the position vacated with Binkley's departure. "We have a hunch Fremont will never be sorry it hired Mal Mackey as football coach," Coxon wrote. He would be proved correct.

When practice began for the Ross football team in September 1950, players saw a different style with Mackey, who was quiet and more cerebral than Binkley (who had been described as loud and driving). John Lewis recalled Binkley as a perfectionist who saw one way of doing things—his way. Lewis remembered a time at practice at Stamm Elementary, next to Harmon Field, when after forty-five minutes of calisthenics, the offense started to run plays. They were running one play, one of their offensive staples, where someone (each time a different player) had done something wrong. And each time, Binkley would say, "Run it again!" The team ran the play until it started to get dark, at which point Mackey sent a player over to the stadium to get a white football so the players could continue to run the play. When day turned into night, the team moved to the stadium and turned the lights on to continue running the play. "My grandmother got to the stadium looking for me!" Lewis said. "We were there until nine o'clock at night. We ran those plays until we got it right." Lewis recalled Mackey as being less intimidating. "He raised his voice every now and then, but he didn't have the physical stature Binkley had."

The Little Giants offense changed with Mackey's arrival, going from a single wing to the T-formation. "Some line players went to the backfield, and some backfield players went to the line," said Dick Sherman, who had graduated in 1950 but still had friends on the team. Lewis said Binkley's single-wing offense was all power. "It was 'Here we come, boys, drop us if you can,'" he said. Mackey's offense was more of a finesse game, which gave Surratt a chance to thrive.

The team won its first three games that year before getting handed a 14–0 loss by Findlay, the same team that handed Ross its only loss in 1949. The

Little Giants hoped to right the ship the following week against Sandusky but made costly mistakes that directly resulted in Blue Streak points as Sandusky beat its oldest rival, 29–7, for the first time since 1946. Bob Markley fumbled for Ross, setting up a Ted Schwanger score. A Charlie Glover fumble set up another Sandusky score, as Jude Thiebert hit a streaking Jim Holzmiller for another touchdown. John Lewis attempted a fake punt from the Ross twelve-yard line, but he slipped, and the Little Giants turned the ball over on downs, setting up a short score by Darrell Hurlburt. Thiebert ran for another score, while Lewis accounted for the only Ross touchdown of the game. Sandusky players carried coach Jeff DeHaven off Strobel Field, while Ross was suffering its first back-to-back losses since 1946. Even with the loss, Lewis and Surratt managed to impress the Sandusky crowd. Among those who remembered watching them was a freshman at St. Mary High School named Charles Wagner. "They were fantastic," said Wagner, who would watch many Ross-Sandusky games in the future.

Ultimately, the Little Giants finished 6–3–1 that year, winning their fifth straight Buckeye League title. It was an acceptable record for most teams, but it was the most losses for a Ross team in one season since 1946. And going into the 1951 slate, it appeared that Ross would have even tougher sailing. Al Coxon wrote in the *News-Messenger* that of the ten-game schedule, five would be tougher than the previous year, three less so and two about the same.

One of the games predicted to be tougher was against Sandusky. Blue Streaks partisans said this was the best Sandusky team since the 1935 squad

The 1951 Ross team went 9–0–1, the first undefeated mark in school history. *Photo courtesy Rutherford B. Hayes Presidential Center.*

The 1951 Ross backfield. *Front*: Center Charles Jones (85). *Back, left to right*: Jerome Surratt (77), Earl Asperger (87), Ron Whitcomb (71), John Lewis (73) and Charles Black (65). *Photo courtesy Van Ness's Time Out Sports Bar.*

that pitched eight shutouts and won the league title, while also laying claim to a mythical state title.

But Ross had two tremendous offensive weapons in its arsenal: Big Thunder and Little Thunder, the nicknames given by Coxon to John Lewis and Jerome Surratt. Lewis, who stood six feet, three inches tall, was the power back. Surratt, significantly smaller, was the scatback. Lewis likened him to Barry Sanders for his speed and cutting ability. "He was so fast," Lewis said of Surratt. "You never got a clear shot at him. Jerome was a hell of a back."

"How great a chapter in the Ross high school football record book will John (Big Thunder) Lewis and Jerome (Little Thunder) Surratt write before they hang up their uniforms on Nov. 16?" Coxon asked.

Behind their running, the Little Giants won their first three games before hosting Findlay. Ross was aching to beat the Trojans, who had handed them their first loss in each of the previous two years—and their only loss in 1949. Ross edged Findlay 25–21, thanks to a 265-yard game from Lewis that included a 90-yard touchdown run from scrimmage, setting a team record. The win made the Little Giants 4–0 going into their matchup with

Ross players Julius Simms (82), Tom McCarthy (86), Jerry Porczak (83) and Jerry Pastorius (81). *Photo courtesy Van Ness's Time Out Sports Bar.*

Sandusky, which was also 4–0 and ranked fifth in the state Associated Press poll. Ross was ranked ninth.

That year, the Sandusky boosters and Gene Jordan, sports editor of the *Sandusky Register-Star-News*, suggested a trophy for the winner of the rivalry game. Ross boosters turned down the idea, calling Sandusky just another game. One went so far as to say that he'd rather see the Little Giants beat Findlay than Sandusky.

In the first quarter of the matchup, Chuck Acierto pulled in a touchdown pass from Jude Thiebert, and Thiebert ran for another score, putting Sandusky up 14–0. Thiebert's score was set up by a Dess DeVeese interception of Ron Whitcomb, which he took to the Ross 23. But in the second quarter, Whitcomb pitched out to Lewis, who then threw a bomb to Jerry Porczak, putting Ross on the board. Jerome Surratt scored in the third quarter to pull the Little Giants within one point, 14–13.

Sandusky got down to the Ross eleven-yard line in the fourth quarter, but the Ross defense let them get no farther, and the Blue Streaks turned the ball over on downs. Ross then moved the ball downfield, grounding and pounding with handoffs to Lewis and Surratt before Lewis went into the end zone for the game-winning score. Coxon predicted that Sandusky wouldn't lose another game that year, writing of a jubilant Little Giants locker room at Harmon Field and Lewis's attitude of gratitude after the game. "Before you shake hands with me, shake hands with that line," Lewis said. "A baby can gain ground behind those boys."

The following week, Sandusky dropped out of the AP top ten, and Ross moved up to sixth—the highest it would get all year. That week, Ross fought Columbus East to a 13–13 tie and then dropped out of the top ten. Lewis said the Little Giants offense was stymied by the defensive alignments thrown at them. "They had defenses we'd never seen before," Lewis said. "They were very unorthodox, and our guys were confused. We were fortunate to tie with them."

But the Little Giants posted wins against Bowling Green, Elyria and Toledo Scott before going into the season finale at Marion Harding.

Ross edged into the top ten again, but the vagaries of the state polls reared their ugly head. Massillon remained at the top of the poll after a loss to Warren, and at one point, the top five teams had at least one loss (Warren had two) while the bottom five teams were all undefeated (Ross had one tie). The Little Giants beat Toledo Scott in the ninth game of the season but dropped from ninth to tenth in the AP poll below Youngstown East—which had just lost to Youngstown South!

Lewis scored three touchdowns in the season finale in Marion, and Surratt and Whitcomb each scored one as the Little Giants clinched their first undefeated season—and Mackey's fourth—with a 32–19 win over the Presidents. Ross won its sixth straight Buckeye League title and finished ninth in the AP and INS polls. The Little Giants' 9–0–1 season marked the first season without a loss in modern school history (the 1897 team went 3–0–2). Sandusky fulfilled Coxon's prediction and didn't lose another game that year, finishing 8–1. Although the Blue Streaks finished out of the AP top ten, they received more first-place votes (two) than Ross did (one).

Lewis and Surratt turned in a season for the ages. Lewis led the team with 1,535 yards and eighteen rushing touchdowns, while Surratt had 1,168 yards and thirteen rushing touchdowns. All told, the two accounted for thirty-four of Ross's thirty-eight touchdowns that year. Their yardage totals put them first and second in the Ross record book at the time. Lewis went on to play football for Michigan State, wooed by the promise of being able to play baseball. Surratt ended up at the University of Detroit but returned to Fremont after less than a year.

In 1952, Coxon started transcribing play-by-play of Ross football games to send to fans and alumni, particularly those who were in Korea or elsewhere in the military during those days of the Cold War. Coxon got local businesses—including Croghan Colonial Bank; Billy's Restaurant, which is still serving breakfasts on West State Street; and, starting in 1955, his insurance brokerage—to sponsor the mailings.

The Little Giants were without Lewis and Surratt in 1952, as both had graduated, but Sandusky faced Ross without Thiebert, who was hospitalized following the Blue Streaks' 13–13 tie with East Liverpool the previous week. Coxon likened Thiebert's absence to the Yankees playing without Allie Reynolds (he had won twenty games that year with a league-leading ERA of 2.06 and 160 strikeouts). Sandusky was 3–0–1 going into the matchup, while Ross was 3–1, coming up short against Lorain and snapping a fifteen-game undefeated streak. The Blue Streaks drove to the Ross 12 in the first period but were stalled, and Ross advanced to the thirty-seven-yard line before Chuck Black broke out off tackle and ran sixty-three yards for a touchdown. It appeared the Little Giants would be poised to score again before the half, but Black fumbled, and Sandusky's Glen Rehfus recovered the ball. The Little Giants had thoroughly pushed Sandusky around in the first half, outgaining the Blue Streaks 215–47 on the ground.

Sandusky put together two sustained drives in the second half, one ending at the eleven but the other culminating in a score by Chuck Acierto, who was carrying the load in Thiebert's absence. Ross punted the ball away but appeared poised to score after Henry Tiller hopped on the ball when Dess DeVeese fumbled the punt. However, at the two-yard line, Whitcomb fumbled, and Sandusky's Jerry Lewis recovered to preserve the 7–7 tie, the first tie in the series since 1944.

Ross finished the season 7–2–1, not good enough to crack the top twenty in either poll, but good enough to win its seventh straight Buckeye League title. Sandusky finished its season 6–1–2.

In 1953, Fremont Ross made a big addition to its schedule. The Little Giants would venture to Massillon to play the Tigers in the ninth game of the season. Excitement built quickly, and even before the Findlay game—the fourth game of the season—plans were being made for a special train from Fremont to Massillon for the game. Coxon cautioned that there were a lot of potentially meaningful games before the November 13 game at Massillon and that they shouldn't be overlooked.

"A couple of losses and instead of a special train, all that will be needed for the Massillon excursion will be a couple of automobiles and a wheelbarrow," he said.

Mackey was nervous going into the Sandusky game, saying that his team appeared overconfident. The Blue Streaks, meanwhile, were sixth in the state—one spot below a Dayton Chaminade team coached by Fuzzy Faust and quarterbacked by his son Gerry.

Before a crowd of more than six thousand—including three scouts from Massillon—Ross started the game with a fumble by Ron Whitcomb. Sandusky's Bucky Laird recovered at the Ross 20, and five plays later, Bill Harple's seven-yard run put the Blue Streaks on the board. Three plays after that, Lester Franks broke off a sixty-two-yard touchdown run to tie the game. Ted Houghtaling threw a touchdown pass to Whitcomb to give Ross a 13–7 lead, and a Charlie Black score in the third made it 19–7, the eventual final.

The game wasn't as close as the score would indicate. Black, who ran for 53 yards on ten carries, outgained the Blue Streaks on the ground by himself. Sandusky managed just 41 yards. Franks led the Little Giants with 135 yards on nine carries. The contest was a physical one, with one player from each team getting ejected. Sandusky school superintendent Carl Mackey almost pulled the Streaks off the field at halftime and forfeited the game—a move the *Sandusky Register* later said could have resulted in the school being kicked out of the OHSAA. In a turn of events, Sandusky was considering no longer playing Ross.

They weren't the only ones. Crestline had left the Northern Ohio League, and Tiffin Columbian was trying to take its place (Tiffin Calvert, Port Clinton and Mansfield Madison also applied for the opening). Tiffin had gone on hiatus from the league for three years beginning in 1950, feeling like it couldn't run with the rest of the teams. In 1949, the Tornadoes were beaten 78–0 by Ross and 81–0 by Findlay in successive weeks. Bowling Green and Fostoria were also considering dropping out of the league. Ross had become the eight-hundred-pound gorilla of the conference.

Vince Sikora of the *Lorain Journal* said the league was so weak that "if you beat Fremont, you win the championship." *Sandusky Register* sports editor John Malcolm said Ross was just too good, while *Bowling Green Sentinel* sports editor Dave Wakefield said Buckeye League games were "breather dates" for the Little Giants, who were becoming a state-ranked powerhouse in the days when there was no divisional breakdown in the polls. There were now three wire service polls in Ohio. That year, the Scripps-Howard wire service, United Press, started making its football rankings. Ross got up to seventh in the INS and UP polls but was eleventh in the AP poll.

Following the win over Sandusky, Ross went to Tiffin and laid a 70–6 beating on the Tornadoes. The Little Giants then beat Bowling Green handily, 44–7, and won 32–14 at Marion Harding to clinch what turned out to be the last Buckeye League title. In fact, Ross won the last eight league crowns.

Now the Little Giants had a date with the Tigers—and a chance to prove themselves worthy of a state title. Both teams were undefeated. Massillon had come off a huge 27–6 win over Warren in front of 21,150 screaming partisans to remain undefeated and atop all three wire service polls. Ross was ranked fifth in the AP poll.

"The whole darn town's agog for the Massillon adventure," Coxon wrote. "Even the Ladies Aid Societies are talking about it."

An estimated 3,500 fans made the trek from Fremont to Massillon—including 1,723 via the Nickel Plate Road, necessitating two special trains departing from Fremont.

At practice the week of the game, the Ross football players got a special visit from Jerome Surratt. His football career was over after a June car wreck had almost killed him, but he urged the team to go out, play with pride and prove they belonged on the same field as the Tigers.

Lester Franks caught a touchdown pass from Whitcomb to give Ross the early 7–0 lead, but that was the only scoring for the Little Giants in Massillon. The Tigers reeled off forty points for the win. The Ross win in the season finale against Toledo Scott was almost anticlimactic, but the Little Giants still finished as league champions, third in the INS poll and sixth in the AP and UP polls. Massillon was the state champion, and Portsmouth was the runner-up in all three polls.

Mackey said after the game that the difference was conditioning, but Massillon coach Chuck Mather was impressed with the talent of the Little Giants. "If Fremont played in a tougher league all year, it could hold its own with anybody," said Mather, who left after the season to become the coach at the University of Kansas. "And I mean anybody."

As it turned out, Fremont got the tougher league the next year. With Fostoria, Tiffin and Bowling Green leaving the Buckeye League, a new home was needed for Ross. It looked to Sandusky, an independent since it was drummed out of the Buckeye League in 1938, and the other remnants of the league, Findlay and Marion Harding. Lorain and Elyria had just left the Lake Erie League in a dispute over sharing receipts, as the Steelers and Pioneers usually had more fans at their games but had to give the visitors a cut of the gate.

The new Buckeye Conference would consist of Ross, Findlay, Marion, Sandusky, Lorain and Elyria—the exact alignment Coxon had suggested in 1950, saying that the league in its current state needed a shakeup.

Bowling Green and Fostoria would join the Great Northern Conference, which split into a blue division of smaller schools that became the Northern Lakes League and an orange division that became the Great Lakes League.

The Buckeye Conference started in 1954, as did the use of face masks in Ohio high school football. The Ohio High School Athletic Association originally granted permission for the use of face masks for players to protect injuries, not prevent them. But there was such a hue and cry from coaches, parents and administrators that the organization relented and allowed anyone to use plastic face masks—a move that didn't sit well with Mackey. "Face masks give a boy a false sense of courage," he said.

Face masks on football helmets were not unheard of but were fairly uncommon. In a game against the San Francisco 49ers in 1953, Cleveland Browns quarterback Otto Graham took a forearm to the mouth, requiring fifteen stitches. Browns coach Paul Brown had required a player at Massillon to wear a face mask to protect him from a broken nose, and he had a face mask made for Graham to wear and continue playing the game. Brown ordered the rest of his team to start wearing them as well. He patented the face mask, and it was soon being mass produced by Riddell. The residuals helped Brown buy a football team in Cincinnati thirteen years later.

The Little Giants began the year with a 25–7 win over Akron South and rallied from a 13–0 deficit to beat Lorain 14–13 in Ross's inaugural game in the Buckeye Conference. The win moved Ross to eighth in the Associated Press poll—which Mackey greeted with some derision.

Massillon, as usual, topped the poll, after wins over Struthers and Canton Lincoln. Warren, second in the poll, beat Cleveland Collinwood and Canton McKinley.

"These polls don't make sense," Mackey told Coxon. "Massillon hasn't played anyone yet, and they're still in first place, while Warren wins two tough games and beats Canton McKinley and is in second place. Too many teams are picked on reputation."

Mackey took special aim at schools from Stark County. Either Massillon or Canton McKinley had won or shared every state title from 1934 to 1943 when they were chosen by popular acclaim, and although the first AP poll was won by Barberton—a school in neighboring Summit County—the next six had been won by Massillon. The INS poll had Massillon, Canton McKinley or Barberton as winner or runner-up every year but two since its start in 1944 as well.

"Those schools in the area have 'em fooled," Mackey said. "They think football isn't played anywhere else."

Coxon was a little more measured in his remarks, saying, "Massillon may have the best team in the state this year, just as it has the last six years, but the Tigers haven't whipped anyone to prove it."

Mackey's screed went out over the AP wire, and Massillon officials reminded him that the Tigers were looking for an opponent for October 7, 1955. Mackey noted that was the Findlay game and said of Massillon, "We'll play 'em ninth." But the Tigers wanted no part of a game against Ross during the week before the big matchup with Canton McKinley, and the Ross-Massillon matchup wouldn't come to pass until 1962.

Ross didn't help its cause with a 0–6 loss to Fostoria, dropping the Little Giants out of the top ten in the AP poll, but Coxon pointed out that football was the only high school sport in Ohio that didn't have any kind of postseason tournament to settle decisively the state championship. "The state poll is the sole method of providing a champion for football," Coxon wrote. "Perhaps the time will come when football will be provided with an equal opportunity to declare a champion through competition on the field."

Coxon suggested a nine-game schedule and a state playoff, with four regional champions squaring off against each other one weekend and then the two winners meeting in a championship game in Columbus. But Coxon offered no method to pick the regional champions, admitting it would be difficult. "And who knows," he said. "The finals in Columbus might grow to a 60,000 gate. The OHSAA might be able to use that kind of money."

Sandusky was undefeated going into the annual matchup

Al Coxon, shown here interviewing Senator Bob Taft (R-Ohio) before the 1952 Republican Convention, was sports editor at the *News-Messenger* in the 1950s and later served as president of the Fremont Ross Athletic Boosters. Coxon, who went on to a lengthy journalism career in Chicago, was an advocate for what became the Buckeye Conference and also used his column to call for a state football playoff system—which was eventually adopted in 1972. *Photo courtesy of Hal Coxon.*

with Ross, which had rebounded from the Fostoria loss to pound Findlay 39–0. The Little Giants were ranked twentieth in the AP poll, two spots behind the Blue Streaks. The game was the same weekend Hurricane Hazel made landfall on the East Coast, sending driving rain throughout northwest Ohio. The Blue Streaks asked to postpone the game until Saturday or Sunday, a rarity for a public school matchup, but Ross insisted on playing the game Friday night—and paid for it, losing 13–0. The loss prompted Coxon to say, "It's the first time a Little Giant team has been whipped by a woman."

Ross quarterback Beebe Schneider fumbled in his own end zone, and Sandusky's Dick Kiser dove on the ball for Sandusky's first score. In the third period, Johnny Bettridge Jr.—whose father's heroics had contributed to a lengthy winless streak for Ross in the Thanksgiving Day matchups a generation earlier—scored as well.

The win moved Sandusky up to tenth in the poll, and Massillon was toppled from its spot at the top of the state rankings after a loss to Alliance. The Little Giants would drop the closing game at Portsmouth, but by then were out of the money in the Buckeye Conference race. Sandusky went 4–0–1 to win the league in its first year, and 7–1–1 overall. But things looked bright for Ross, which finished 7–3 in what was supposed to have been a rebuilding year.

"The outlook for 1955 is just as rosy as it is for the Rose-Bowl bound Buckeyes," Coxon wrote after the season.

And in the final poll rankings, Massillon was pronounced champion by the AP, United Press and INS. Mansfield Senior was the runner-up in the UP poll, while Alliance was second in the AP and INS polls. The Aviators and Tigers both finished 9–1 (with Massillon's lone loss coming to Alliance), yet the Tigers were once again state champions.

But while optimism reigned for Ross in 1955, as the Little Giants returned fourteen lettermen, coach Mal Mackey tempered it with the knowledge that Ross faced a difficult schedule. Both the Little Giants and Blue Streaks were undefeated going into the showdown at Harmon Field, and although it was midseason, the stakes were high. "Besides a heap of personal satisfaction, the game has extra significance," wrote the *Toledo Blade*. "The winner is almost certain to emerge with statewide recognition, and there's the Buckeye Conference championship, too."

The crowd was estimated between 7,500 and 8,000, as all reserved seating sold out in advance. The Little Giant defense was tasked with stopping Larry Corso, who averaged 9.4 yards per carry going into the game, and Jim Schwanger, who averaged 6.2. The Blue Streaks, on the other hand, planned to contain running back Jim Tiller.

Ross managers Mike O'Farrell and Rick Schleibner called the temperate climate for the Sandusky game—a welcome change from the monsoon of the year before—"Tiller weather," and Tiller got the Little Giants on the board when, from the Sandusky 31, he ran off left tackle, broke loose, shook off a tackler at the eight and hit pay dirt. Beebe Schneider's kick made it 7–0. But with 9:30 left in the second quarter, Corso rumbled twelve yards for what turned out to be Sandusky's only score of the game. The kick sailed wide, and Ross held a 7–6 lead. With 4:05 left in the first half, Tiller took a handoff from Schneider at the 25 and this time ran off right tackle, scoring again to make it 14–6. Fullback Haldon Black also scored for Ross, bulling in from a yard out in the fourth quarter. This time, Schneider's kick missed, but Ross had an insurmountable 20–6 lead and ended up handing Sandusky its first loss of the year by that score. Tiller finished with 151 yards on eighteen carries.

Despite the win, Ross actually dropped two spots in the AP poll, prompting further comments from new *News-Messenger* sports editor Dan McCarthy. Although McCarthy noted that northwest Ohio, the area that would know Ross best, was particularly bereft of Associated Press subscribers (and thus, voters), there was no reason for Ross not to get the attention fans felt it deserved.

The following week, Ross beat Elyria, which, coupled with a Lorain loss to Sandusky, gave the Little Giants the lead in the Buckeye Conference. After that, the Little Giants got enough votes—including one first-place vote—to jump to twelfth in the AP poll, eleventh in the UP poll and just out of the top ten in the INS poll. One fan wrote to McCarthy and cited the Dunkel Index, a mathematical formula created in 1929 for college football teams, saying that Ross was seventh in the state. Murphy explained that the formula took into account the level of opposition and the number points scored against that opposition, creating a rating on a team's power and not its reputation.

Ross then went to Lorain to play the Steelmen, with travel no doubt aided by the James W. Shocknessy Turnpike, which had opened the month before. Ross's 28–0 win clinched a share of the Buckeye Conference and moved the Little Giants to tenth in the AP poll. It was just the third time in the previous seven years that the Steelmen were blanked. The following week, Ross clinched the outright league title with a 30–12 win over Marion Harding. The Presidents were the first team that season to score more than once against the Little Giants. With a win against Toledo Scott to move Ross to 9–0, the Little Giants moved up to sixth in the AP poll. Ross was one of five unbeaten teams at the top of the Associated Press poll, with the others being Canton McKinley, which was ranked first in the poll; Massillon, second; Columbus East, third; Toledo DeVilbiss, fourth; and Ross sixth.

Mansfield, with one loss to Springfield, was fifth. Mansfield and Massillon had tied earlier in the season.

The 1951 Ross team went 9–0–1, but no Ross team had ever gone unbeaten and untied. The Little Giants would face Portsmouth in the season finale. The Spartans were 3–6 going into the game and had been shut out twice already.

But Portsmouth gave the Little Giants all they could handle, getting on the board first before Schneider hit Tiller down the sideline for a twelve-yard touchdown pass. The Spartans scored again, but Ross answered back with a Black seven-yard scoring run. He also scored the extra point to make it 14–13 in the third quarter. Schneider's interception on the ensuing drive set Ross up at midfield, and the Little Giants got some breathing room with a three-yard touchdown by Tiller and a one-yard run by Black. Ross won 28–13 to clinch its first 10–0 season in school history. The Little Giants ended the season fourth in the AP poll and seventh in the UP and INS polls. Ross got ten first-place votes in the AP poll. Massillon, which finished as runner-up to Canton McKinley, got none.

"Well, it was a great season," the play-by-play records said. "These Fremont kids deserve plenty of credit and praise. They're unbeaten and untied, and we're proud of 'em!"

A poem, "Our Undefeated Football Team of 1955," was written by Fremont's poet laureate, Edwin Erchenbrecher:

> *Ten football games without a loss*
> *Compiled by our own Fremont Ross*
> *Those Little Giants sure came through*
> *They really were a mighty crew.*

About the Sandusky game, it said,

> *Then our ancient rival from old Sandusky*
> *Tried us out and they are always husky*
> *But Tiller's two, Black's one and Schneider's kicks*
> *Gave us twenty points to the Blue Streak's six.*

The Little Giants' 1956 season began with a 38–7 win over Cuyahoga Falls. The game marked a return home for Bob Shaw, who was head coach of the Black Tigers. He was the first of two Ross alumni coaching Little Giant opponents that year. His teammate Art Burton coached Fostoria, which visited Harmon Field and also loss to Ross as the Little Giants moved their win streak up to thirteen games. Ross got its fourteenth straight win with a 53–6 drubbing of Findlay and was undefeated and ranked fourth in all three major polls going into the Sandusky game. The Blue Streaks were 2–1–1.

The Blue Streaks were starting a drive when Ross's Ken Stull intercepted a pass by Blue Streaks quarterback Roland Unckrich at the Sandusky forty-yard line and returned it to the thirteen-yard line. Tiller covered twelve yards on the first play, and Schneider dove over for a touchdown. Larry Corso returned the ensuing kickoff from the twenty-yard line to the thirty-five before the ball was jarred loose by a hit from Bill Smiley. Schneider dove on the ball for the recovery and ran it in from fifteen yards out to give Ross its second touchdown of the game. Unckrich connected with Corso for a twenty-seven-yard touchdown pass to pull within five, 12–7, but in the second half, Tiller ran for a touchdown and passed to Clarence Glover for another as the Little Giants rolled to a 25–7 win.

The following week, Ross went to Elyria and came home with a 37–6 win but without Mal Mackey, who suffered an apparent heart attack at halftime.

"Every player among them in the Ross second half action and coaches alike, forgot victory strings, state ratings and records of other sorts, and went out to win for Coach Mackey," McCarthy wrote. The Little Giants would be without the services of Mackey for the rest of the season, as

Ross coach Mal Mackey (left) talks to his assistants, from left: John Ihnat, Jack Decker, Paul Raines and Robert Seele. *Photo courtesy Van Ness's Time Out Sports Bar.*

Seele, who was offered the job but didn't want it in 1950, became the interim head coach.

With a Mansfield victory over Massillon, the Little Giants were able to slip into second in the AP and UPI polls after the Elyria win, but the win over Lorain dropped them to third behind Canton McKinley and Mansfield. Ross beat Marion Harding to clinch its second straight Buckeye Conference crown and finished out its second straight 10–0 season with wins over Cleveland John Marshall and Toledo Scott.

With another undefeated season came another poem by Erchenbrecher:

> *The fifth in line was proud Sandusky*
> *And those Blue Streaks are always husky,*
> *But our boys put four touchdowns over*
> *Schneider two, Tiller one and one by Glover*
> *25 to 7 our favor, man alive*
> *We were halfway through, and then there were five.*

In 1956, the annual McKinley-Massillon game was billed as a de facto state championship game, something that stuck in the craw of Mackey, who challenged the winner to a game afterward, and Coxon, who helped Mackey agitate for it. Even though Coxon no longer worked for the *News-Messenger*, he continued to tout Ross athletics (he would serve as president of the Ross Athletic Boosters) and wrote to Don Wolfe, the sports editor of the *Toledo Blade*.

"I don't say we could beat McKinley," Coxon quoted Mackey as saying. "That's not the point. But it would be a fine game, it would be fun to get ready for it, and our fans would love it. Both schools would make money and it might set a precedent for the post season playoff every year."

The Little Giants had to settle for being named runner-up in the AP and INS polls—to Canton McKinley, which was also named state champion by the United Press, with Mansfield Senior as runner-up. It was—and still is—the highest poll ranking by a Ross team in school history.

Ross was without Jim Tiller in 1957, as he had graduated and was playing football at Purdue University. But Mal Mackey was back and slimmed down after his heart attack. The Little Giants kept winning, starting the season fourth in the Associated Press poll, and once again were undefeated going into the Sandusky game. The Blue Streaks were winless, but the matchup gave credence to the old saw that records didn't matter in rivalry games.

The Little Giants covered sixty-four yards in eighteen plays, culminating in a three-yard plunge off left tackle by Richard Baker. John Level booted the extra point—the only successful extra point all night—to give Ross a 7–0 lead. On the ensuing drive, the Blue Streaks covered seventy-five yards in fourteen plays, including a twenty-four-yard sprint down the left sideline on the first play of the second quarter by Willie Nesbitt. Donovan Bryant missed the extra point. Level scored for Ross to push the lead to 13–6, but Ed Bettridge blocked the extra point. Waudell White ran twenty-two yards to pull back within one, 13–12, but that turned out to be the final score. Ross escaped to push its winning streak to twenty-five games but dropped to fifth place in the Associated Press poll.

Ross won its next four games to run its winning streak to twenty-nine games, with only Toledo Scott standing between the Little Giants and their third straight 10–0 season. But nobody told the Bulldogs, who took a 13–0 lead into the fourth quarter. Level ran for a touchdown and passed for another to Chuck Houdeshell, and Ross salvaged a 13–13 tie. Their winning streak ended at twenty-nine games, but they were still undefeated in three straight seasons, finishing seventh in the AP poll. That year, United Press and International News Service merged to form United Press International, and Ross finished sixth in the new UPI poll. The AP poll compiled votes from sportswriters and broadcasters, while UPI polled high school coaches.

After the 1957 season, there was another poem, which this time didn't rhyme "Sandusky" and "husky."

Our ancient enemy from Lake Erie
Came next and made things "not so cheery,"
Those Blue Streaks are always tough
In fact they almost had enough
To upset us but still we won it
By just one little point, "we done it."
Baker and Level each scored a TD
And Level's plunge was enough, believe you me,
The battle was tough, both ambitions were keen,
But Sandusky lost it, twelve to thirteen.

In 1958, longtime Ross assistant Bob Seele had moved on, but among the new faces on Mackey's coaching staff was team trainer Jim Gruden, who would go on to coach at Heidelberg and Muskingum and serve as an assistant coach at Notre Dame. His son Jon, born in Sandusky while his father was a Little Giants assistant, would go on to coach the Oakland Raiders and lead the Tampa Bay Buccaneers to a Super Bowl victory.

Ross opened the season sixth in the preseason UPI poll and would host Cincinnati Purcell, a Catholic school that featured a junior named Roger Staubach (spelled Stauback in the *News-Messenger*) as defensive back and halfback. Purcell beat Ross 12–0, the first shutout loss for the Little Giants since the 13–0 loss to Sandusky in 1954. Ross's undefeated streak was over at thirty, but it still had a sixteen-game conference winning streak. That ended three weeks later, as Ross led a 12–0 lead slip away in a 14–12 loss to Findlay. It turned out to be a bleak year for Ross, which went 1–7–2. In 1959, things were only a little better, as the Little Giants went 2–8. Worse yet, after a sixteen-game Buckeye Conference winning streak, Ross started a ten-game league losing streak.

Mackey would coach Ross through the 1966 season, but after 1957, he would win just one more league title—shared with Sandusky—and have one season in which the Little Giants won more than six games. He remained the Ross wrestling coach as well, having started the program there in 1953, and was active as a wrestling coach until his death from a second heart attack on January 26, 1972, at the age of fifty-three.

Ross alumnus John Lewis played on two Michigan State Rose Bowl teams, catching a touchdown pass in the 1956 game against UCLA. *Photo courtesy Michigan State Athletic Communications.*

On December 28, 1958, Ross graduate Bob Shaw could be found on the sidelines at Yankee Stadium as the receivers' coach for the Baltimore Colts. The Colts, with just their second winning season since the team's founding five years earlier, met the New York Giants in the NFL Championship Game. According to Mark Bowden in his book *The Best Game Ever*, Shaw's duties also included watching Giants practices from adjoining tall buildings. After a stellar career at Michigan State that saw him play in two Rose Bowls, John Lewis was drafted by the Colts. But he was also drafted by the U.S. Army, and Uncle Sam won that fight.

The NFL had been plodding along since its beginning in 1920 and in 1950 had absorbed three teams from the All-American Football Conference: the Browns, the San Francisco 49ers and the Baltimore Colts (those Colts folded after a year in the NFL; the Colts playing against the Giants were an NFL expansion team). For the first time in its existence, the NFL was on solid financial footing and enjoying relative stability. The 1958 game was notable for two reasons. First, it was the first game in NFL history to go into overtime, with the Colts prevailing 23–17 on an Alan Ameche one-yard run. Second, it put the NFL on the map. Newspapers throughout Ohio referred to the high school game as "king football," and towns would stop on a dime for college football games, but the professional game hadn't really taken hold until an estimated 45 million people watched John Unitas, Raymond Berry, John Mackey and Ameche lead the Colts over the Giants in what has since become known as "The Greatest Game Ever Played." The pro game was starting to take its role in the national consciousness.

CHAPTER 6

SANDUSKY'S SENSATIONAL '60S

In 1958, Ross was the king of the hill, unbeaten in its last thirty games (including a twenty-nine-game winning streak) and having won three straight Buckeye Conference titles. Mal Mackey had talked up the previous year's freshman team as the equal to those teams led by Jim Tiller.

One of the new faces in the Buckeye Conference was Sandusky coach Ben Wilson, a graduate of Dover High School and Heidelberg College. Wilson was the center for Dover's undefeated 1942 team and had served as a head coach at Wellston and Mount Vernon. While at Wellston, he compiled a 31–6–1 record, and at Mount Vernon he compiled a nineteen-game win streak in two undefeated seasons for the Yellow Jackets. Wilson was hired by John Tabler, who had become athletic director in 1957 after a decade at Sandusky as an assistant football coach and track coach.

Among Wilson's assistants would be Bob Seaman, who had played for DeHaven. After graduating from Sandusky (his father was the Sandusky school superintendent), Seaman went on to Kent State University. His collegiate athletic career was cut short by a knee injury, but he earned bachelors and master's degrees and returned to his alma mater, where he served as an assistant coach for DeHaven. Seaman served as offensive line coach for Wilson.

And while Ross was losing its opener to Purcell, the Blue Streaks were pounding Cleveland Rhodes 50–6. "Act one of a nine-act play entitled 'Win With Wilson' went off without a hitch," wrote John Malcolm in the *Sandusky*

Register. "And that's putting it mildly." Ray Young ran for three touchdowns, Ernie Delaine ran for two and caught a touchdown pass from Jim Gill and Waudell White ran for another.

Both teams were 1–3 going into the annual grudge match, but once the game started, the teams weren't evenly matched, as Sandusky plowed to a 46–0 win. Jim Gill threw two touchdown passes, one to Young and one to Walt Williams, and Willie Nesbitt, Young, White and Williams each ran for a score. Nesbitt also recovered a fumble for a score. The worm was turning.

Sandusky finished the season 4–5. The four wins were as many as the Streaks had won in the previous two years combined and included the first victory over Mansfield since 1945. The *Sandusky Register* went so far as to say that Sandusky was the best team with a losing record in the state. Ross, on the other hand, was listing. Its 1–7–2 record prompted the *Register* to remark, maybe with a little *schadenfrude*, "How the mighty have fallen."

The following year, Sandusky got out to a 26–8 halftime lead, thanks to touchdowns by Dave Scott, Jon Jackson and Tim Ziemke, but Ross clawed back to pull without two points in the third quarter, 26–24. Ben Espy's fourteen-yard run put the Blue Streaks on top for good, 32–24. The win was Sandusky's fourth of the year—equaling the Blue Streaks' win total from the previous year. Jim Ohms, Lloyd Booth and Denny Stine scored for Ross. The game was a Pyrrhic victory for Jackson, who tore ligaments in his left knee and was lost for the season. The Blue Streaks finished 6–3 and wouldn't have a losing record again until 1974.

After just two years at Sandusky, Wilson left for Warren Harding. Coaching the Panthers had become one of the preeminent jobs in the state, as Harding had proven itself the equal of Massillon, Canton McKinley and Alliance, regarded as state powers by fans and poll voters.

Among the applicants for the Sandusky job was Earle Bruce, who served as a coach at Ohio State while still a student after an injury ended his playing career. Bruce had compiled a 28–9 record as coach at Salem High School and had previously interviewed for the Toledo Waite job. Bob Reiber, who grew up with Bruce in Maryland and was one of his assistants in Salem, accompanied him on the trip and recalled Bruce saying as they drove past Sandusky, "They just got a new high school built, and it's beautiful." And when the coaching job came open, Bruce applied for it, viewing Sandusky as a program on the rise. "I knew they had great talent," he said. "It was set up to be a success."

Not only were the Streaks starting to get better, they were starting to get noticed. The initial UPI poll had them ranked eleventh, and they were sixth in the AP poll. After a 22–0 win over Elyria, the Blue Streaks rose to sixth in the UPI poll but then dropped to eighth the following week despite a 44–0 win over St. John's (Jackson, Michigan). But they had moved up to fourth and were 5–0 going into the Ross game. The Little Giants were doing better as well, riding a three-game winning streak that included a 32–0 win over Findlay to end Ross's ten-game league losing streak.

Sandusky players Ben Espy and Judge Scruggs, nicknamed "Bruce's Galloping Gooses" by the *Register*, were hanged in effigy by Ross players before the game. The *Register* viewed it as a compliment, writing, "Since such treatment is usually accorded only the very best, it's expected the Streak swifties will be extra anxious to show the Little Giants and their followers how good they are tonight."

More than fifty years later, Bruce continued to rave about their speed—as well as the speed of the team in general. Espy and Scruggs were also tremendous athletes, he said. "They were both twelve-foot pole vaulters," said Bruce, who pole-vaulted once—when he had to in a physical education class at Ohio State. Reiber said Bruce's track skills were in running, noting that he was a Maryland state champion in the 100-yard dash.

Scruggs scored two touchdowns. Espy scored none but scored a couple of two-point conversions as the Blue Streaks rolled to a 32–0 win. McRay Smith also scored a touchdown, and Bruce was able to get two scores from a sophomore who wasn't even starting, Steward Williams. Williams would become a big part of the Blue Streaks' success in the following two years. The win, the Blue Streaks' third shutout of the year, moved Sandusky up to third in the UPI poll. The Blue Streaks remained fourth in the AP poll.

In Week Nine, Sandusky beat Findlay 34–20 and got help from Ross, which upset Marion Harding—itself just two years removed from a UPI state title—to clinch at least a share of the Buckeye Conference for Sandusky. The Blue Streaks won the inaugural conference crown in 1954 but had been shut out first by Ross's dominance from 1955 to 1957 and then by the Presidents. And as luck would have it, Harding was hosting Sandusky for the season finale. A Blue Streaks win would give them an outright league title and their first undefeated and untied season since 1935.

Harding and Sandusky were scoreless after three quarters, but Ron Johnson hit Sandusky's Tom Rudolph to force a fumble, which was recovered by Harding at the Sandusky nineteen-yard line. It took seven plays, but Harding finally crossed the goal line on a pass by Larry Sims to Larry Imbody. The Presidents' defense held on to preserve the 6–0 win. Harding and Sandusky would share the league title. It would turn out to be the only game in the 1960s in which Sandusky failed to score a touchdown.

"They played a hell of a defensive game," Bruce said. "We were predictable as hell. I looked at the film."

"That probably cost us a state championship," said Reiber, who had come with Bruce from Salem to Sandusky.

Among those in the stands was a student and football player from Otterbein University. Gene Kidwell played football for the Cardinals and had lettered at Miamisburg High School (he would eventually enter his high school's athletic hall of fame). One of his Otterbein teammates, a Sandusky native, had gone on and on about how good the Blue Streaks were, and he had to see for himself. He sat through the freezing rain to watch them lose their only game of the season, but two years later, he would be part of Bruce's coaching staff in Sandusky.

The 1961 schedule featured a new opponent for Sandusky. The Lorain City Schools had grown so big in the postwar suburbanization and baby boom that a second high school was opened. Its namesake was Ernest J. King, a Lorain native who rose to the rank of fleet admiral in the U.S. Navy and served as commander in chief for the U.S. fleet during World War II. Lorain Admiral King—as well as Mansfield Senior—would become full members of the Buckeye Conference in 1962, bringing membership in the league to eight schools. Charles Wagner, by then a staff writer at the *Register* and known to one and all as Butch, said the conference alignment was nearly perfect, in his view, spanning from Mansfield and Marion in Central Ohio to Lorain and Elyria in the Cleveland suburbs and Findlay and Ross getting toward Toledo. And right in the middle of them all was Sandusky.

That year, the Blue Streaks were 5–0 going into the rivalry game, while Ross was 4–1, with a 28–12 loss to Toledo Waite in the second week of the season as its only blemish. Both teams were undefeated in the Buckeye Conference at that point as well. "When we drove into Fremont, you could feel the electricity," Reiber said. "Everybody was so fired up that week. Teachers might have just as well forgot about teaching."

By then, Williams had become the featured back for Sandusky. UPI called him the state's top fullback, and he had scored three touchdowns the week before in a 46–14 rout of Toledo Whitmer. Williams got 118 yards on twelve carries but was held scoreless. In fact, the Blue Streaks were held scoreless until the waning moments of the game, when Jim Glick hit Don Rather for a meaningless touchdown pass in a 24–6 loss. "It was an upset, but they played well," Bruce said. Jim Ziemke scored two touchdowns for Ross, and Steve

Frontz added another. The win put Ross firmly in the Buckeye Conference driver's seat, with Sandusky being forced to play catch-up.

The Blue Streaks, who kept pace in the league, caught a break when Ross lost 36–8 at Marion Harding. The Little Giants would have two more non-league games, but Sandusky's remaining schedule included one more Buckeye Conference game—against the Presidents, in fact. It was an opportunity for some redemption—and some payback. Sandusky made the most of it with a 22–20 win, as Steward Williams ran all over the Presidents, piling up 228 yards. The win made the Buckeye Conference title a three-way split between Ross, Sandusky and Harding. The crown was an outlier for the Little Giants, the only one they won between 1957 and 1972, and the last one won by a Mal Mackey–coached team. But it represented a passing of the torch between Marion, which had won or tied each of the previous four league titles, and Sandusky, which would have a virtual stranglehold on the Buckeye Conference through the 1960s.

"Most important aspect of this outcome was Sandusky's emergence from an also-ran status going into the game to a one-third holder of the Buckeye Conference title coming out," the *Register* wrote.

But when the 1962 polls started, it was the Little Giants finally getting their due, starting the season atop the Associated Press poll, ahead of the Blue Streaks (sixth), as well as Niles McKinley, the defending AP poll champions, and Massillon.

Ross ascended to the top spot by virtue of an 8–7 win in the season opener at Massillon. The Tigers had won the 1961 UPI poll and finished second to Niles in the AP (the Dragons were runners-up in the UPI poll). Sandusky led Parma 14–0 but was forced to scramble for a 20–20 tie in its opener. By the time the annual meeting rolled around, both teams remained undefeated, Ross at 5–0 and Sandusky at 4–0–1. Reserved tickets for the game at Harmon Field sold out in twenty minutes, as both teams were state ranked. Ross was third in the AP poll, and Sandusky was seventh. The game was billed as a matchup of fullbacks, both of whom were nursing injuries. Ross's Jack Ziemke was coming back from a separated shoulder, and Steward Williams was hobbling around on a sprained ankle.

Ziemke provided what turned out to be the only score for Ross, a touchdown run with fifteen seconds left in the third. By then, the game was all over but the shouting, as Sandusky won 30–6. Williams scored once, as did Ernie Gast, and quarterback Dave Milne found Don Rather for two touchdowns, including a sixty-yard bomb on the fourth play from scrimmage to set the tone for the game.

Sandusky rose to third in the AP poll and fourth in the UPI, while Ross dropped out of the top ten altogether. The Blue Streaks followed the win at Ross with an 8–6 victory over Harding. Williams had twenty-three carries for 154 yards, including an 8-yard touchdown run in the third to tie the game. Ernie Gast's two-point conversion turned out to be the margin of victory. It was the first time since 1954—the first year for the Buckeye Conference and the last time Sandusky won the league title outright—that the Blue Streaks had beaten Ross and Harding in the same season.

Sandusky kept on winning, over Marion and Findlay, and held a 20–0 lead over Elyria going into the fourth quarter. But the Pioneers scrambled back to tie the game at twenty, creating a logjam at the top of the conference standings between Admiral King and Sandusky going into the last game of the season. The Blue Streaks and Admirals were both undefeated when they met in the season finale—which turned into the Steward Williams Show. Williams ran for 222 yards and five touchdowns on twenty-seven carries in a 38–8 rout to give Sandusky the undisputed Buckeye Conference championship and its first undefeated season since the Blue Streaks went 8–0–1 in 1938—the team's last year in the old Buckeye League.

The Blue Streaks were fourth in the final AP poll, but that year, the *Sandusky Register* started carrying Conley ratings, a formula taking into account strength of schedule, game location and field conditions, among other variables. The Blue Streaks finished first in the Conley ratings. By comparison, Toledo Central Catholic—named state champion in the AP and UPI polls—was ranked sixth according to Conley. But it was all talk until some kind of playoff system could be set up. "I would love to have had a playoff," Bruce said. "I think it would have worked well for us."

Two weeks after the Sandusky loss, Ross lost 24–16 to Lorain Admiral King, putting the Little Giants two games back in the new eight-team Buckeye Conference. Ross won its last two games, against Mansfield and Marion Harding, but despite an 8–2 finish ended up out of the money in the league and out of the top ten in both polls. It was the best record Ross would have in the 1960s.

New on the coaching staff that year was Gene Kidwell, who was coaching eighth grade football and swimming and teaching science. Kidwell was recruited to Sandusky by Bob Seaman, an Otterbein alumnus. Kidwell was coaching with Seaman's son Bob, who had been an assistant football coach at Sandusky going back to Jeff DeHaven. "The program was really flourishing when I got here," Kidwell said. "It had very few, if any, weak points. We had big kids, fast kids, strong kids."

But raw talent only goes so far. Kidwell said the team also had a young, eager coaching staff—with organization directly attributable to Earle Bruce. "We had so many good athletes and so many young coaches that were eager to be involved with the program." At his first practice for eighth grade football, Kidwell saw 110 boys out. "Everyone wanted to be part of the program," Kidwell noted. Although he was the eighth grade coach, he was considered a varsity assistant and could be found on the sidelines Friday night or in the stands at another Buckeye Conference game scouting a future opponent. At practices, he would run the scout team as well.

It was a different time then for sports news. It was primarily newspaper coverage (the press hadn't yet given way to the media), and Kidwell and other assistants would be collecting articles from other newspapers and sending letters to other coaches and media members, touting players for all-conference and all-district teams and touting the team for votes in the AP and UPI polls, at the time the only way to determine football state champions.

He said one of the reasons for the Blue Streaks' success through the 1960s was that they continued to get those kinds of numbers—enough to field FOUR teams for seventh grade and as many for eighth grade—throughout the decade and retained a lot of those that they got.

The 1963 football preview in the *Sandusky Register* said there was talk that the Blue Streaks were due for a letdown. Although the team returned thirteen lettermen, just three of them were starters. "Can it be so?" the *Register* asked.

The 1963 Sandusky High School football team. That year was Earle Bruce's last as Blue Streaks coach, and his staff included four assistants who would also go on to become head coaches. Bob Seaman succeeded him as coach at Sandusky and Massillon, John Behling would spend a year as Ross coach before returning to New Philadelphia and serving as coach there, Gene Kidwell would serve as Sandusky head coach and Tony Munafo would serve as coach in nearby Huron. *Photo courtesy Gene Kidwell.*

"It could be, but it's far too early—far, far too early—to write them off as a contender for a repeat Buckeye Conference championship."

With an eight-team Buckeye Conference, every team would have three non-league games at the beginning of the schedule and then seven conference games. Sandusky found a new opponent to open its slate, Erie (Pennsylvania) Tech Memorial. The school proved to be a punching bag, losing 44–0, the first of four shutouts Sandusky would pitch that year. The second came the following week with a 32–0 win over Cleveland John Marshall. After a 52–22 win over Garfield Heights, the Blue Streaks had outscored their opponents 128–22 in the three non-league games.

The league slate began with Marion Harding, and fears of a letdown proved decidedly premature. Bill Yeager scored three times, and Gary Miller and George Williams each scored twice in a 48–0 drubbing of the Presidents. A fourth Yeager touchdown was called back, but on the following play, Cecil Weatherspoon scored. After a 52–6 win over Lorain Senior, the Blue Streaks found themselves atop the Associated Press poll, occurring in part of the brief interlude where the *Register* dropped its UPI membership for the AP.

The Blue Streaks' reign at the top was short-lived. Sandusky needed a seventy-eight-yard touchdown run late by Tim Stokes to preserve a 12–12 tie against Findlay, but the tie still toppled the Blue Streaks to fourth in the AP poll (fifth in UPI) and, more importantly, out of the Buckeye Conference lead. The game the following week, against Elyria, had suddenly become a must-win—which Sandusky did, 26–14, to take a half-game conference lead going into the Ross game.

The Little Giants had only two wins that season, but one was a 12–6 triumph over the Findlay team that had vexed Sandusky two weeks earlier. Would Ross give the Blue Streaks fits? Sandusky more than handled the Little Giants offense, holding Ross to just five yards in the second half and no first downs. George Williams—Steward's brother—and Bob McClellan each scored two touchdowns, and Tim Stokes scored another in a 34–0 pasting. Sandusky went on to beat Admiral King 23–14 to go into the season finale against Mansfield Senior. The Tygers were the last team to beat Sandusky, 28–14 in 1961, and the rest of the league did whatever they could to make history repeat itself. The *Sandusky Register* reported that the Blue Streaks were being "gang tackled," as every team in the league except Elyria sent film of their game against Sandusky to Mansfield.

It didn't matter. In front of a home crowd that included alumni celebrating the twenty-fifth anniversary of the undefeated 1938 team, the Blue Streaks beat Mansfield Senior 52–8 to clinch the fourth straight Buckeye Conference title and second straight undefeated season for Sandusky.

The 1963 Blue Streaks went 9–0–1, scoring 375 points, good for a third-place poll finish behind Niles McKinley—then in the middle of a forty-eight-game winning streak—and Massillon. Earle Bruce had put together an impressive four-year stint at Sandusky. He was undefeated at home and had won a league title every year, and twice he was recognized as coach of the year. Bruce attributed his success to the talent—and speed—of the players he coached and the support he and the team received from the community and the school district.

Bruce was quickly snapped up by Massillon to succeed Leo Strang, who was named coach at nearby Kent State University. Bruce said he initially turned down the job, but a call from his mentor, Ohio State coach Woody Hayes, changed that. "You better go there," Hayes told Bruce. "You know what you're passing up? That's the best high school football job in the country!" After Massillon, Bruce joined Hayes's staff at Ohio State and ultimately succeeded him as head football coach.

The Blue Streaks looked inward for a replacement, promoting Bob Seaman to head coach. Bruce was confident the team was in good hands and would continue to get better.

Fremont Ross also made a key hire—albeit one behind the scenes—in 1964. John Titsworth stepped down as athletic director, and Superintendent Robert Oldfather, the Ross football coach in the 1930s, had to find a replacement. He looked beyond the current coaches and hired an alumnus, Dick Sherman, for the position. Sherman had bachelor's and master's degrees from Bowling Green State University, where he served as a graduate assistant to Doyt Perry with, among others, Sandusky High School graduate Bill Mallory.

Although he was a Ross graduate, Sherman saw Sandusky as a program worth emulating. "They were our big rival, and we had to bring ourselves up to their standards," he said. He started a weightlifting program and also began a ball-boy program for the high school football team in which elementary school students would spend their time at football practice and develop an interest in the sport and the team. "The athletes on the field might not have been winning, but they were still idols to the ball boys," Sherman said. "It was a good program, and it generated a lot of interest." And many of those ball boys in the 1960s became players—and stars—for the Little Giants in the 1970s.

The *Elyria Chronicle-Telegram* compared Sandusky to the New York Yankees in the 1964 football preview. But while the Yankees' dynasty was wobbly (the

The 1964 Sandusky High School football team. *Photo courtesy Gene Kidwell.*

Bombers had lost the previous year's World Series and would advance to the World Series and lose again that year before sinking into the second division), the Blue Streaks showed no signs of letting up.

"Outside of Massillon and Niles, no Ohio high school built a greater winning tradition than did Sandusky during the Earle Bruce regime," wrote Pete Swanson. "The Streaks know how to win and expect to win, important plusses for Coach Bob Seaman's first team."

The 1964 season began with Niles McKinley's forty-eight-game win streak snapped. The Dragons lost 14–8 in Earle Bruce's debut as Massillon head coach, in front of more than thirty-one thousand fans at the Rubber Bowl in Akron. Sandusky beat Erie Tech in its opener to run its unbeaten streak to twenty-three games, then the second-longest streak in the state behind Lima Shawnee. After Shawnee lost to Lorain Central Catholic in Week Three and the Blue Streaks rallied from an 8–8 tie to beat Toledo Libbey 19–8, Sandusky had the longest unbeaten streak in the state at twenty-five games.

The streak ran up to twenty-eight games before Elyria came to Strobel Field. The Pioneers beat the third-ranked Blue Streaks 32–6, ending Sandusky's overall, league and home unbeaten streaks and putting Elyria in the lead in the Buckeye Conference race. Sandusky dropped to ninth in the UPI poll, while the Pioneers went from seventh to third and even got a vote for first place.

Sandusky started its next win streak the following week at Harmon Field. The Cleveland Browns—including Sandusky and Bowling Green State University graduate Ed Bettridge—were tearing up the NFL, thanks in no small part to running back Jim Brown. The Blue Streaks had a Jimmy Brown of their own, a five-foot-seven-inch "mighty mite" who ran for both touchdowns in a 16–0 shutout of the Little Giants. Brown scored two touchdowns in a six-minute span in the third quarter. Ross, meanwhile, was held scoreless, crossing midfield just twice in the game. Elyria beat Marion Harding 40–0 to remain in the lead in the Buckeye Conference. Going into the season finale against Mansfield Senior, Sandusky needed to win and also needed Lorain to beat Elyria for a fifth straight conference title. The Blue Streaks held up their end with a 48–6 win, and it appeared they would get help, as Lorain led Elyria 14–0 at one point. But the Pioneers clawed back for a 23–14 win and the Buckeye Conference title. Sandusky finished 9–1, good for seventh in the final UPI poll and sixth in the AP. Both poll titles were won by Massillon, where Earle Bruce had accomplished the only thing that had eluded him in Sandusky: a 10–0 season.

Seaman, like many people at the time, called the Buckeye Conference the toughest week-after-week schedule in Ohio. UPI poll voters saw fit to give the championship to league member Marion Harding in 1958, but in 1964, Seaman said he didn't think Sandusky would win a title if it was left up to poll voters. "I don't think a Sandusky team will ever be rated No. 1, no matter how good the team is," he told *Cleveland Plain Dealer* reporter Paul Baumgartner. "That Stark County should dominate is planted in the people's minds."

The next year would prove him wrong.

Sandusky opened the 1965 season with Lakewood and won 16–0. To prove Sandusky had entered the ranks of the elite, people were concerned that Sandusky didn't win by enough. "Sandusky High's football team didn't have the 'laugher' its faithful have come to expect of opening games," the *Register* wrote. Meanwhile, Ross battled Springfield South to a 6–6 tie.

Fans got the laugher the following week, as the Streaks rolled 42–0 over John Marshall. The Lawyers got three net yards of offense and no first downs. Also that week, Ross beat Cleveland West 36–0, giving coach Mal Mackey his 100th career win. He remains the only Ross coach to cross that milestone.

Both Ross and Sandusky kept on winning. Ross ended its non-league slate with a 16–8 win over Toledo Bowsher and beat Mansfield, Marion, Lorain and Findlay to rank ninth in the UPI poll going into the Sandusky game. The Blue Streaks beat Toledo Woodward crushed Marion 51–14, and the score wasn't even that close. Sandusky had a 51–0 lead in the third before Seaman called off the dogs. The Blue Streaks followed that win with decisive wins over Lorain (44–0), Findlay (30–6) and Elyria (26–0). Sandusky was second in the AP and UPI polls, both of which had split that year.

Since the INS poll's inception in 1944, all the polls were for just one top-ten list of schools throughout the state. The poll belonged to schools that were high achievers but also had a reputation as a football power. Massillon had won ten of the first eighteen state titles, and two schools named for William McKinley—in Canton and Niles—accounted for two more each. The polls were also biased toward bigger schools. Starting in 1965, the Associated Press awarded two poll championships, for Class A (big schools) and Class AA (small schools).

For Sandusky fans, the Ross game was "the greatest show in football," the *Register* said. For Fremont fans, it was nothing shy of a nightmare, as quarterback Brian Healy found end George Garrett three times for touchdowns in a 54–0 rout. Arry Keyes caught an option pitch from Healy for a forty-eight-yard touchdown run and after Ross was forced to punt on the ensuing possession ran that back seventy-two yards for a score. Cleveland Dickerson and Healy also ran for scores as Sandusky found itself alone in the lead for the Buckeye Conference title. Ross, then in second, spiraled out of the race with successive losses to Elyria and Admiral King to end the season with three straight shutout losses.

Despite the resounding win over a ranked opponent, Sandusky didn't budge in either poll the following week, as all signs pointed to a Massillon repeat as state champions. "The Tigers look like a sure bet for another perfect season and an accompanying state title that seems to go to all unbeaten Massillon teams," UPI Ohio sports editor Bob Grimm wrote in his weekly story with the poll.

Much as Ross and its fans found itself a decade earlier, Sandusky rooters felt slighted by a poll system that conferred rankings on teams based on reputation, if not always on talent. Former sports editor Mel Harmon, writing a regular column in the *Register*, suggested that battles waged in the polls

Sandusky alumnus Cleveland Dickerson would go on to play college football at Miami University. *Photo courtesy Miami University Athletics.*

were "a losing proposition for Sandusky High." "We'll make a wager that coaches in love with Massillon or the coaching staff might well toss a vote or two in favor of Sandusky if they had the opportunity to see the Blue Streaks in action," he wrote after the Ross game.

Harmon noted that Massillon had more games that offered chances at statewide exposure, while Sandusky's league affiliation limited it to three non-league games, all at the beginning of the season. He pitched a "dream Buckeye Conference" that would form two divisions: a north with Sandusky, Fremont, Findlay, Harding and Lorain, and a south with Massillon, Canton McKinley, Admiral King, Elyria and Mansfield Senior. The winner of each division would meet in a championship game.

Sandusky had clinched the Buckeye Conference championship the week before its finale with Mansfield Senior. A Streaks win over Admiral King and a Ross loss at Elyria ensured the league crown would belong to Sandusky alone, but there was still plenty at stake against Mansfield Senior. A win would give the Blue Streaks their first 10–0 season in thirty years. Fans also held out hope—slim though it might be—that a win would give them a state title. The Blue Streaks were still ranked second in the UPI poll.

Sandusky took care of its business, rolling up 521 yards in a 48–0 win over Mansfield Senior. It was the Blue Streaks' fifth shutout win of the year, as the Tygers got just three first downs. Massillon had beaten Mansfield 38–12 earlier that season, making the Tygers the only common opponent for both teams, and coach Gary Prahst felt confident in giving his opinion. "Sandusky is by far the better team," he told the *Register*. "Sandusky's backs are better than Massillon's backs. Healy is a better quarterback than Massillon's Dave Sheegog…Cleveland Dickerson is better than Massillon's fullback, and the two halfbacks are far superior to Massillon's halfbacks." Prahst said he'd put Sandusky at the top of his ballot for the UPI poll. (The AP poll was done by sportswriters and broadcasters; high school coaches voted in the UPI poll.)

And the mail delivered something that would make high school football fans throughout Ohio positively giddy. Earle Bruce, who was the athletic director and coach at Massillon, sent a letter to Sandusky athletic director John Tabler, Seaman and the *Register* with open dates in 1966, 1967 and 1968—all in September to accommodate Sandusky's non-league schedule. "If there is any interest in Sandusky to schedule Massillon, we would like to open negotiations as soon as possible, and I am sure game arrangements and financial reward would be good for both teams," Bruce wrote. "It is the policy of Massillon football to schedule top competition from outside our league area and Sandusky can surely compete against Massillon."

"It would make the season complete if we would be named No. 1 in the state," Healy said after the game.

After the game, Seaman started politicking, reminding poll voters of Sandusky's continued success and dominance. The following Tuesday, the *Register* crowed that Sandusky was the United Press International champions. The Blue Streaks had gotten a total of 379 votes, including 18 first-place votes. Massillon was second with 16 first-place votes and 375 total votes. It was the closest margin in the twelve years that UPI, going back to its days as United Press, had been conducting the Ohio poll. The Blue Streaks were runners-up to the Tigers in the AP poll. Kidwell said the UPI poll meant more in Sandusky, since the *Register* was a UPI subscriber. A total of seventeen players from that team got some kind of scholarship to play football in college, Kidwell said.

Massillon had finished the season 10–0 to make Bruce 20–0 in two years at Massillon. The game against Sandusky never came to pass. Bruce left Massillon after two years (he remains the only undefeated Tigers coach) and became an assistant coach for Woody Hayes at Ohio State before ultimately becoming his successor. Because picking a Sandusky coach had worked so well for the Tigers, they did it again, hiring Seaman to serve as head coach.

The Blue Streaks went to their bench, making assistant Bob Reublin the new head coach. Reublin, a former player and graduate assistant for Doyt Perry at Bowling Green State University, was a backfield coach for Seaman in 1965. And although Sandusky graduated twenty-one varsity players, they had a sophomore team coached by Kidwell that went 7–1. Whether it was players or coaches, the Blue Streaks weren't rebuilding; they were reloading.

"There is nobody on this squad that doesn't think we can win 10 games this year," Reublin said before the 1966 season started. He stated the team's goals as a 10–0 season, a Buckeye Conference championship and a state title. The team controlled its destiny for the first two goals but would need help from poll voters for the third.

Sandusky started the season with a 16–6 win over Lakewood and then, before a crowd at Strobel Field that included Ohio governor James Rhodes, beat Cleveland East 38–8. When the first polls were released, after Sandusky beat Toledo Woodward 46–0, the Blue Streaks were tied for first in the UPI poll with Warren Harding and second to Steubenville in the AP poll. Sandusky beat Lorain but dropped to second in the UPI poll behind Steubenville. Big Red topped the AP poll as well after knocking off Warren Harding.

Ross was having a mediocre year and was 3–4 going into the Sandusky game, with wins over Toledo Rogers and Cleveland West in its non-league

The 1966 Sandusky High School football team. *Photo courtesy Gene Kidwell.*

schedule and its only Buckeye Conference win coming over Marion Harding. Sandusky had dropped to third in UPI and fourth in the AP poll going into the Ross game, which Butch Wagner, who had become sports editor for the *Register* in 1964, laid at the feet of other Buckeye Conference coaches.

A total of five league coaches voted in the UPI poll: Reublin, Mackey, Mansfield's Gary Prahst, Hal Paul of Findlay and Pete Riessen of Admiral King. Wagner said Reublin regularly voted, and Paul voted that week, but the others hadn't lately or had turned in their ballots too late. Wagner went on to say that there are six other coaches in northwest Ohio who didn't seem to be supporting Sandusky and that Sandusky wasn't able to get the kind of statewide support that a program like Steubenville or Niles McKinley would get.

Whatever ill will Sandusky might have had it took out on Fremont—and then some. The Blue Streaks set a Buckeye Conference scoring record with a 74–0 drubbing. It was the fourth straight shutout of Fremont by Sandusky, which scored on eleven of its fourteen total offensive possessions and torched the Fremont defense for 677 yards of total offense. Amison, who was described as "the back that carries the mail" by James Rhodes when he saw the Blue Streaks beat Cleveland East, had six carries for 151 yards— averaging more than 25 yards per carry—and scored two touchdowns. Ed Williams also scored twice. Reublin pulled his starters early, as his second and third teams got playing time in the bloodletting.

"I wanted to beat Fremont bad, but not that bad," Reublin said in the next day's *Register*. It was the third-worst beating Sandusky had ever put on an opponent, after a 98–0 win over Huron in 1914 and a 78–0 win over Norwalk in 1935. Even a year later, talking to the *Plain Dealer*, Reublin

The cover of the 1966 Ross-Sandusky game program.

remained sheepish about the win. "We honestly didn't want it to happen that way," he said. "Our execution was near perfect. We were scoring when we didn't want to. It's a game I'd rather just forget."

Wagner remembers a harsh crowd at Harmon Field, with some fans throwing eggs at the Blue Streaks as they took the field. He also remembered George Garrett, catching one of his three touchdown passes from Bill Deming and getting hit late in the end zone by a Fremont defender into a snow fence.

Among those in the stands was Jon Kerns. His father Russ was a Fremont native but lived in Helena during his high school years and graduated from Gibsonburg High School. Russ Kerns got a World Series ring as a bullpen catcher with the 1945 Detroit Tigers, who defeated the Chicago Cubs in the last World Series they've appeared in to date.

It was the first Ross game for Jon, who would go on to be the radio voice of the Little Giants on WFRO-FM. He was eight years old, and he recalled looking up at his father and saying, "Are they all going to be this bad?"

A pair of seventh graders from Bidwell Avenue—the same street where Big and Little Thunder grew up—was also watching the game. They played football for Fremont Junior High School. Chuck Lindsey recalled Tommie Liggins looking at him and saying, "If we ever get up here, that's never going to happen to us. We're going to bring the team back." Liggins wanted nothing more than to play Fremont Ross football, and he was determined to have Lindsey on the field with him. Lindsey's older brothers Eddie and Walt played football, but he didn't want to go out for football because he didn't like getting hurt. So Liggins gave him a choice: either get beat up on the football field, or get beat up by him. Lindsey joined the team.

It was the worst beating Mal Mackey had ever taken, and it was the last time he'd lose to Sandusky. After a 3–7 season, Mackey would hang it up as football coach, an ignominious end to a lengthy and successful tenure.

The Blue Streaks caught a break in the polls, as Bob Seaman's Massillon team beat Steubenville 12–0 to topple Big Red from the top of the poll—and reinstall Sandusky there. The Blue Streaks capped off the season with a 34–0 win over Mansfield Senior to go 10–0 for the second year in a row. After the loss to Elyria in 1963, Sandusky had put together a twenty-three-game winning streak. The Blue Streaks had beaten Lorain Senior and Elyria by identical 20–12 scores, but no other Buckeye Conference team had gotten within thirty points of the Blue Streaks that year. The Catholic school in Sandusky, St. Mary, completed its first 10–0 season in school history in 1966, giving Sandusky claim to being the football capital of Ohio.

Now, the Blue Streaks and their fans would await the following Tuesday's *Register* with the results from the last UPI poll. The Blue Streaks were defending poll champions, with another 10–0 season under their belts. Surely they'd win another UPI championship. "I expected it," Wagner said.

But fans were surprised—and not pleasantly so—to find out that the Blue Streaks had dropped from second to THIRD in the final poll. Columbus Bishop Watterson appeared out of nowhere to take the top spot in the AP and UPI polls, while Niles McKinley took second. A total of 10 points separated first from third in the UPI poll, with Watterson getting 394 points, Niles getting 392 and Sandusky getting 382. The Blue Streaks got thirteen first-place votes. The Dragons got fourteen, and the Eagles got ten—but they were the ones that ended up atop the poll "in what local fans termed the greatest robbery since the Brinks caper," Wagner said.

"Too bad there isn't a district playoff," Mel Harmon lamented. "Bet our Blue and White would leave no doubt in the fans' minds who is CHAMPION of Ohio's Class AA grid powers again this year." Still, the Blue Streaks and Panthers were feted with a parade November 19—that included a float with an outhouse painted as the "ofishall UP and AP voting booth."

"We had the same team back, which made it hard not to win a state title," Reiber said. Kidwell said the 1965 state championship team and the 1966 team that should have won a state title were two different kinds of teams. The 1965 team had a stronger defense, but the 1966 team had more speed and a better offense. But the 1966 team had accomplished something unprecedented in school history: the seniors on that team had never lost a game, dating back to seventh grade.

But it was politics, not play, that decided football championships. "It was a political football," Wagner said. "Massillon just owned the polls."

In 1967, Fremont Ross and Sandusky had one thing in common: they were both coached by former Sandusky assistants. Mal Mackey was replaced by John Behling, a New Philadelphia native and Columbus North graduate who was an assistant to Earle Bruce at Sandusky and then at Massillon. It was Behling's first head coaching job, but he had applied for the Sandusky job when Seaman left. Instead, the Blue Streaks hired Reublin, who returned as head coach in 1967 and picked up right where the Blue Streaks left off.

Sandusky rolled its win streak up to twenty-four with a 28–0 victory in the opener over East Chicago (Indiana) Roosevelt. Since Oberlin and Louisville lost their openers, the Blue Streaks owned the longest active winning streak in the state for the second time in three years. And for the second time in three years, they saw the streak broken, this time at twenty-five games with a

19–16 loss to Toledo Woodward in the Blue Streaks' final non-league game. It was Reublin's first loss as Sandusky head coach.

The Blue Streaks rebounded to start the Buckeye Conference season with shutout wins over Marion and Lorain Senior, but Findlay got out to a 13–0 lead over Sandusky. The Blue Streaks scored twenty-four points in the fourth quarter to hold on for a 24–13 win and then edged Elyria 14–13 to go into the Ross game with a 6–1 record. Ross was holding on to a 4–3 record. The Little Giants won their non-conference slate against Rogers, Cleveland West and Bowsher, but their only Buckeye Conference win came against Findlay the week before the Sandusky game.

The good news was that for the first time in five years, Ross got on the board against its oldest rival—on a Jim Daniels run set up by a Mike McGuire interception of Sandusky quarterback Dan Miller. But the Little Giants still lost, 36–6. The win, along with a Findlay win over Admiral King, clinched a seventh Buckeye Conference title in eight years for Sandusky. Williams scored three first-half touchdowns, two rushing and one on a twenty-nine-yard pass from Miller. Ike Brown and Miller also ran for scores. Future University of Michigan player and Cleveland Brown Thom Darden picked off Ross quarterback Rusty Williams to set up Brown's score.

Sandusky finished the year with wins over Admiral King and Mansfield Senior, rolling its conference winning streak up to twenty-four games as it won its third straight Buckeye Conference title and ended up finishing fifth in the UPI poll.

Behling resigned after just one year as Ross coach, so in 1968, Fremont Ross hired Chuck Shuff, who had coached Oak Harbor for the preceding three seasons, going 16–13–1. Shuff had previously served as an assistant to Ben Wilson, the former Sandusky coach, when he was at Warren Harding. Sherman still remembers sitting in Shuff's living room discussing the job with him. "He was very interested," Sherman said. "We were a bigger program." Within the next six years, Sherman would be responsible for the hiring of the next three Ross football coaches—each of them successful in the role.

The Blue Streaks blew through their non-league schedule in 1968, outscoring opponents 60–6. They avenged their only loss of the previous three years with a 12–0 shutout of Woodward but stumbled into the Buckeye Conference season with back-to-back losses to Marion Harding and Lorain Senior. Harding had lost twenty-six of its last twenty-eight league games and hadn't beaten Sandusky since the teams shared the league title in 1960. The Presidents took a 7–0 lead into the final two minutes of the game. Sandusky scored, but quarterback Rich Deeter was stopped on a potential game-

The cover of the 1968 Ross-Sandusky game program.

winning two-point conversion to preserve the win. The 18–8 loss to Lorain marked the first time in one hundred games that Sandusky lost back-to-back contests. "The 'Monsters of the Seaway' label the Blue Streaks have carried in the 'Sensational Sixties' has evaporated," Wagner wrote.

Sandusky got back on track with a 12–6 win over Findlay but lost again, 27–6, to Elyria, effectively taking them out of the Buckeye Conference race going into the Ross game. The Little Giants under Shuff were rebuilding. They had one win, a 14–6 decision over Toledo Bowsher, but four of their six losses had come by eight points or fewer.

It wasn't the massacre Sandusky fans had come to expect and Ross fans had come to dread, but the Blue Streaks won their seventh straight over Ross, 13–3. Ike Brown ran fifty-four yards to score on the first play from scrimmage for Sandusky, but the Blue Streaks couldn't manage another score until Lino Venerucci stepped in front of a Ross pass for a forty-three-yard interception return. It was the third of three picks Sandusky had in the game. The other two were by Steve Rogers. Sandusky finished the season with wins over Admiral King and Mansfield Senior. A 7–3 record was nothing to be ashamed of, but for Sandusky and its fans, used to contending for league and state titles for the better part of the past decade, it was nothing to be particularly proud of either. It was the first three-loss season for Sandusky since 1959, and oddly enough, the losses were to the same three teams: Marion Harding, Lorain and Elyria.

From 1960 to 1968, the Blue Streaks had gone 79–8–3, with a state title, seven Buckeye Conference crowns, two 10–0 seasons and two other undefeated seasons. It was the most successful era since Bob Whittaker coached in the 1930s, and it was a confluence of factors: talented athletes, smart coaches and a community that got solidly behind the team. "We were fortunate to have all that talent in one era," Wagner said.

CHAPTER 7

1969

THE TURNING POINT

As the 1969 football season dawned, there was no reason to believe that anything was going to change between Ross and Sandusky. The Little Giants hadn't beaten their rival since a 24–6 win in 1961, and since then, had only scored fifteen points against the Blue Streaks.

Ross had dominated the Buckeye Conference from 1955 to 1957, going 29–0–1 and winning nineteen straight conference games, but had only won twenty league games since. Expectations weren't high for second-year coach Chuck Shuff, who was coming off a 1–9 season.

"It's doubtful Chuck Shuff can bring them back to respectability," Butch Wagner wrote in the annual high school football preview in the *Register*.

News-Messenger sports editor Roy Wilhelm was a little more optimistic, saying, "A respectable year in 1969 could lead to even better things in the 1970s."

But it was entirely possible that 1970 could dawn with closed schools in Fremont. The *News-Messenger* Pigskin Preview featured a full-page ad urging Fremont City Schools voters to approve a school levy in a special election on September 9 after it had failed in May. If the levy failed this time, the district would have to close schools until after the first of the year, when new funds became available.

The Buckeye Conference title was expected to be slugged out by the Blue Streaks and Elyria. Sandusky was coming off a 7–3 season, and the Blue Streaks were so good that that was a down year for them. Their three losses in 1968 were more than all of the six previous seasons, which included 10–0 seasons in 1965 and 1966. Assistant Gene Kidwell became the new head coach at Sandusky. Reublin had been lured to Miami of Ohio by coach Bill Mallory, himself a Sandusky graduate. The staff Mallory compiled also included another former Sandusky assistant, Dick Crum. Reublin would go on to serve as assistant coach at Miami, Colorado and Bowling Green. That summer, Mallory put on a clinic at Kenyon College. Among those who listened to him extol the virtues of Mallory's new Offset-I offense was Chuck Shuff, who realized that the plays Mallory talked about were similar to those the Little Giants coaches were considering, so Shuff implemented the Offset I—calling it the Y offense—that fall at Ross.

The Little Giants opened with a loss and tied Cleveland West 26–26 in Week Two. Two weeks later, Ross outlasted Mansfield Senior 24–22 for its first win of the year. The levy failed on September 9 but was put on the November ballot. It would literally be the last chance to keep the schools open in Fremont. They were scheduled to close on November 14.

The Blue Streaks, on the other hand, won their first six games of the year before losing a 13–12 slugfest to Elyria, dropping Sandusky to sixth in the state Associated Press poll the week before the Ross game. Wilhelm said the loss would either make the Blue Streaks "mad as hornets or it could slow them down for the week."

Wilhelm predicted a Sandusky win, as did Wagner, who went so far as to predict a 36–8 victory, saying, "The Blue Streaks bounce back with their highest point total of the year."

"They weren't giving us any chance," Dick Sherman said. "But we thought we could give them a game."

Kidwell said that game-planning for Ross was intense, even though the Little Giants had just one win. The Buckeye Conference, regarded as one of the toughest leagues in the state, demanded complete preparation. "If you didn't play good, basic, tough, hard-nosed football, you were going to get your clock cleaned," he said.

Reiber, who remained on the Sandusky staff through the 1960s, said both sides took the rivalry seriously—even with Sandusky's recent winning streak against Ross. "There wasn't any bigger game," he said. "The rivalry was there no matter what. It was like Michigan-Ohio State. You win that game, the other ones don't count."

A pep rally behind Ross High School (on what is now the infield of the high school track) showed Lindsey how important the Ross-Sandusky game was to fans. He remembered a plane flying overhead trailing a banner that read, "Let's start a new era; let's beat Sandusky."

More than seven thousand fans packed into Strobel Field for the game. Elmer Lippert took the opening kickoff from Ross to the Little Giants' 27, but Ross was off sides and kicked again. This time, Lippert returned the kickoff for a touchdown, his second kick return for a score that season.

Ross was down but not out. On the ensuing drive, the Little Giants were able to cover sixty-eight yards on five plays, the last being a forty-seven-yard touchdown pass from Jim Werling to Tommie Liggins. The sophomore was already the leading scorer in the Buckeye Conference. Robin Young's two-point conversion gave Ross an 8–7 lead.

Then Sandusky mounted a drive of its own, covering sixty-

Tommie Liggins. *Photo courtesy Rutherford B. Hayes Presidential Center.*

one yards on eleven plays, capped off with a Lippert eighteen-yard run. Mark Deming's second extra point of the day made it a 14–8 Sandusky lead.

After the teams traded punts, Sandusky was driving almost to midfield. Kidwell said that Buckeye Conference teams were always fundamentally sound, so coaches had to look for an angle. "You knew you were playing a team with athletes just as good as you were," he said. "You knew you were coaching against coaches as smart as you were. The preparation came down to finding one thing that worked." And Kidwell thought he found something that would make the difference when he drew up a throwback play. "The offensive coordinator up top didn't call that play," he said. "I called that play." The Streaks had practiced the play all year but had never run it in a game. Ben Chapman threw the ball downfield…to Ross sophomore Chuck Lindsey. "Chuck read it the whole way," Kidwell said. "He had to be fifteen yards away from the receiver when the ball was thrown, but he covered that ground."

Lindsey ran the interception back for a touchdown to tie the game. "I was in the right place at the right time," he said. That was true in several senses. Lindsey said if it was up to him, he wouldn't even have been on the field, having gotten injured on the previous play. "Tommie Liggins wouldn't let me leave the field."

Liggins was dragged down just shy of the goal line on the two-point conversion to keep the game tied at fourteen but would go on to score on an eighteen-yard touchdown run to put the Little Giants up 20–14.

Sandusky would score twice within a minute—both times by Lippert—to take a 27–20 lead. Deming missed the extra point.

With 4:53 left to play, the Little Giants were punting away. Sandusky's Ray Scott fumbled it, and the Little Giants got the ball at the Sandusky 48. Facing fourth and ten at the twelve-yard line, Werling scrambled around the backfield before heaving it to Liggins, who scored to pull Ross within one. Young's two-point conversion gave Ross a 28–27 lead with forty-two seconds left to play.

Everyone in the stands was tense. Bruce Gulde, a Ross lineman who was watching the game on crutches on the sidelines, recalled seeing cigarettes being lit in the stands to the point where it looked like Strobel Field had been overtaken by a flock of lightning bugs.

The Blue Streaks took the Ross kickoff to midfield and then advanced to the Ross twenty-six-yard line. A touchdown pass from Chapman went through Scott May's hands, and Sandusky was forced to attempt a forty-two-yard field goal. Deming's kick was long enough, and the fans watched it sail over the left upright.

"In my mind, it was good," Kidwell said forty-four years later.

But the referee disagreed, calling the kick no good. Kidwell said it was the type of kick that could have been called either way, but for the first time in eight years, Ross had beaten Sandusky—and it had done so at Strobel Field.

The Blue Streaks put up stunning numbers. Ben Chapman was seven-of-ten passing for 101 yards. He had thrown two interceptions—both to Lindsey—and his last pass to May was his only incompletion of the game. Lippert finished with 206 yards on twenty-seven carries and had scored all four of Sandusky's touchdowns.

"We were just not mentally prepared for Fremont," Kidwell said after the game. "They came to play and wanted to win more than we did."

The Blue Streaks dropped from sixth to eleventh in the state AP poll, but Wagner noted that the win could have an effect on another kind of voting for Fremont. "The shocking triumph could be just enough to swing the pendulum the other way when the voters go to the polls in 10 days to decide on the school operating levy which must be passed or have the schools close November 14," he wrote.

And he was right. Voters passed the levy by a margin of 7,160 to 3,947, and local residents and business owners lined up to pay their taxes in advance to ensure that the schools would stay open.

The two big heroes for Ross that day, Liggins and Lindsey, were both sophomores. Someone pointed out to Shuff that he'd get them for two more years. "I don't mind that at all," he said. Liggins was the eldest of seven children and would be the first of four boys to distinguish themselves playing for the Little Giants.

But more than that, Shuff was going to see a serious influx of talent into the Fremont Ross ranks. Among the freshman at Ross that year were two men who would go on to fame and fortune playing football in high school, college and the NFL: Bob Brudzinski and Rob Lytle. Lytle called the win miraculous, saying it ended almost a decade of people wondering if Ross and Sandusky should play each other because the rivalry had become so lopsided.

"The older I got, the more I understood that was a turning point in Fremont Ross football," Lindsey said of the 1969 game in the *News-Messenger*.

"That was the turning point of our program," Sherman said of the game. "From there, things just started snowballing."

"That gave us faith we could beat Sandusky," Lindsey said.

If the preceding decade was the Sensational '60s for the Blue Streaks, the upcoming one would be the pride era for Fremont Ross. Since that 1969 game, Sandusky has never put together a winning streak against its oldest rivals longer than three games, has never scored more than thirty-five points against Ross and shut out its rivals just four times. (By comparison, Ross has shut out Sandusky ten times since the 1969 game). The overall record in the series is 53–46–8 in favor of Sandusky, but Ross has gone 28–14–1 against the Blue Streaks since 1969.

"In the end, there was a beginning," Wilhelm wrote in his game story. "The dawning of a new day for the Little Giant, who could look to the future and smile."

CHAPTER 8

THE 1970s

LYTLE AND BRUDZINSKI, A PUNISHING TANDEM

As the 1970 season dawned, Fremont Ross found itself loaded with talent—some of which hadn't even reached its full potential.

Sophomore Rob Lytle and junior Tommie Liggins would be running backs for Ross. Bob Brudzinski would see some action at end, and Chuck Lindsey would play split end on offense and defensive back. Ross lost the opener against Toledo Rogers, won four straight and then lost two heading into the matchup against the Blue Streaks at Harmon Field.

The Little Giants drew first blood with a Mike Ruland field goal in the first, but Sandusky marched down the field on the ensuing possession to score. Bob Jackson, running for his life from the Fremont defense, hit Bob Crabb on a thirty-six-yard touchdown pass and then connected with Scott May on a two-point conversion. Ross fumbled, setting up Sandusky nearly at midfield. Five plays later, Clarence Wooten ran it in from four yards out, and Sandusky then had a 16–3 lead, which it carried into the half.

The Little Giants scored a touchdown thanks to Bill Burkett in the second half, but the Blue Streaks ate up most of the fourth quarter with a sixteen-play, ninety-five-yard drive, culminating in a score by Mark Deming to put the game away at 23–9. Sandusky went on to finish the season 9–1 to win the Buckeye Conference and finish seventh in the AP and eighth in the UPI polls, which had split to three divisions that year.

Ross dropped to 4–4 and ended up finishing the season 5–4–1. However, even that was an accomplishment, as the Little Giants won more games that year than in the previous two years combined.

Bob Brudzinski. *Photo courtesy Rutherford B. Hayes Presidential Center.*

Also in 1970, former Sandusky coach Bob Seaman ascended to the top spot at Wichita State—in the worst way possible. Seaman was an assistant to former Blue Streaks coach Ben Wilson, who had been named Shockers coach in 1969. The team was flying in two planes to a game at Utah State. The planes stopped for refueling in Denver, and the Gold plane—named for one of the school's colors (the other plane was the Black plane)—crashed after hitting some trees due to pilot error. Of the forty people on board, thirty-one died, including Wilson and his wife, Helen. Seaman was on the Black plane, which landed safely. The Gold plane included the head coach and starting players, while the Black plane carried assistant coaches and reserves. Seaman became the new head coach.

Fortunes had changed so quickly at Fremont Ross that in 1971, Chuck Shuff said the goal was nothing less than an undefeated record. He believed he had the talent to do it as well, calling his backfield the best he'd ever coached. Those Little Giants had an "L" of an offense, with quarterback Ben Lopez, running backs Rob Lytle and Tommie Liggins and Lindsey, who was the team's leading receiver but had some carries out of the backfield as well. The Ross-Sandusky game was back at the end of the schedule for the first time since the Thanksgiving Day matchups in the 1920s and 30s. Ross was 8–1 going into the game at Strobel Field. The Little Giants won 32–0, the first time the Blue Streaks had been shut out since 1965 and the first Ross shutout win over Sandusky since 1947.

Rob Lytle ran for 115 yards, and Tommie Liggins ran for 127 yards. Both finished the season with 1,000 yards rushing, just the second time in Ross history that happened. The first time was when John "Big Thunder" Lewis and Jerome "Little Thunder" Surratt did it in 1951.

The Little Giants finished 9–1, tied for second in the league with the Blue Streaks. Lindsey said that Ross team might have been the best high school football team ever. "We had so many weapons," he said, adding that he felt like the Ross teams he played for in high school had more talent than the teams he encountered when he played football at Bowling Green State University. Lindsey said the problem with the team was that it was one-dimensional, throwing just one hundred passes the entire season.

Rob Lytle. *Photo courtesy Rutherford B. Hayes Presidential Center.*

Elyria, which included a two-way player named Les Miles—a Michigan alumnus now the head coach at Louisiana State University—beat Ross 15–7 at Harmon Field and went undefeated to win the league crown. Lindsey said the win over Sandusky took some of the sting out of losing to Elyria, which would be named state runner-up in the AP and UPI polls, behind Warren Harding.

Liggins finished his Fremont Ross career with 2,579 yards rushing, good at the time for third in school history, and went on to play at the University of Cincinnati. Lytle's season total of 1,212 yards was good for fourth most in school history. He averaged more than 8 yards per carry. The Little Giants finished seventh in the AP and UPI polls. The wire service polls had been used for years to determine state champions, but starting in 1972, their importance would diminish. The Ohio High School Athletic Association started a football playoff, dividing the schools into three classes: big schools, medium schools and small schools. Four teams, one from each region, would make the playoffs, which consisted of state semifinals a week after the season ended and then state finals a week after that—just as Al Coxon had suggested a generation earlier.

Unlike other sports in Ohio, not every football team would get a chance to play a playoff game. Jack Harbin, a cash register repairman and volunteer football coach at Westlake High School, had started assembling a points system in the 1960s, taking into account second- and third-level points based on wins by a team's opponent. For the first time, strength of schedule would matter.

Harbin made his pitch to the OHSAA, which did a trial run in 1971 and then used it in 1972 (and ever since) to determine the state's playoff entrants. Harbin, who died in 2002, took no reward for his efforts, but ever since, teams enter the playoffs based on their Harbin points totals.

Massillon won the AP and UPI state championships in 1970, but the Tigers, who so often stood between Ross and Sandusky and a poll championship, haven't won an OHSAA state title since playoffs started in 1972.

The week before the 1972 Sandusky game, Rob Lytle tore up Findlay's defense for 209 yards, pushing his season total over 1,000 yards and making him the first Ross running back since Jim Tiller to put up back-to-back 1,000-yard rushing seasons. Lytle's achievement was even more impressive considering that he played only twenty-eight out of forty quarters in the season. All told, he gained 1,253 yards on 154 carries, averaging more than 8 yards a carry.

Lytle rolled up 118 yards on twenty-two carries for the Little Giants and scored his nineteenth and twentieth touchdowns of the season to lead Ross to a 14–0 victory that gave them a share of the Buckeye Conference with Elyria. Ross went 9–1 again, losing to Lorain Admiral King, and finished the season fourth in the Associated Press and UPI polls. The defense gave up just 64 yards of offense to the Blue Streaks. But in what would become a sad tradition for Ross, they sat home while watching Bowling Green go to the playoffs. Sandusky finished a game behind Ross at 8–2.

Ross coach Chuck Shuff was recognized as the league and district coach of the year, Lytle was the AP district back of the year and Brudzinski was the lineman of the year. Lytle, Brudzinski and Tom Pitts were recognized all-Ohio.

Greenville native Bob Marker had moved to Fremont to become sports editor of the *News-Messenger* in 1973. He had heard that the Buckeye Conference was one of, if not the toughest leagues in the state. Since full league play began in

1955, the league had always had at least one team finish in the top ten of at least one of the wire service polls—and for the previous three years, that team had been Ross. "And it was everything I thought it would be," Marker said. He saw Lytle and Brudzinski play in all-star games, but his first football season turned out to be Shuff's last in Fremont.

Brad Borden returned at quarterback, and the Little Giants won their first eight games before getting upset 28–20 by Findlay in Week Nine. The Little Giants were sniffing blood coming into the rivalry game at Sandusky. Borden threw a touchdown pass to Mike Matthes, his ninth touchdown reception of the year, and Tim Smith ran for three scores in a 24–8 Ross victory. The win gave Ross a 9–1 finish for the third year in a row and clinched the school's second straight Buckeye Conference title—and the first outright in seventeen

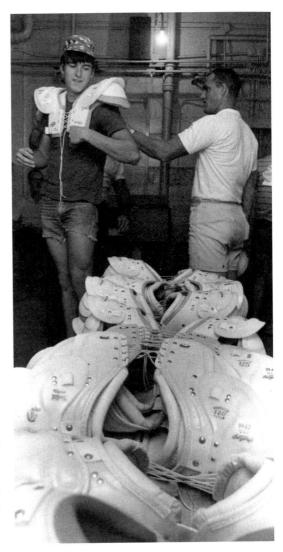

Ross coach Chuck Shuff fits Bob Brudzinski with shoulder pads. *Photo courtesy Rutherford B. Hayes Presidential Center.*

years. The Little Giants finished the year seventh in the AP poll and sixth in the UPI poll. In six years, Chuck Shuff had gone 35–23–2 for the Little Giants, but he was headed to Massillon now to coach the Tigers, following in the footsteps of Paul Brown, Lee Tressel, Earle Bruce and Bob Seaman. Shuff's predecessor at Massillon, Bob Commings, was a Youngstown native

The 1973 Fremont Ross coaching staff. *Photo courtesy Rutherford B. Hayes Presidential Center.*

and University of Iowa alumnus who left Massillon to coach his alma mater. Shuff was the third Buckeye Conference coach poached away by the Tigers, after Sandusky coaches Bruce and Seaman.

When Marker started in Fremont, he had told Ross athletic director Dick Sherman, "If you lose a coach, I know a couple good ones." Marker recommended Tom Hollman, a St. Mary's native with an impressive track record. Hollman spent three years as an assistant at Sidney and three years as a head coach at Greenville, going 26–2–2, including a 10–0 season. In his career, he had coached championship teams and four undefeated seasons. Sherman made a trip to Greenville to research the coach. The reports on Hollman were almost universally positive—with one exception. Sherman had a booster tell him indignantly that Hollman threw him out of practice one day. But Sherman didn't view that as a character flaw. "In fact, I thought that was a plus," Sherman said. "I thought, 'This is the kind of football coach I'd like to have.'" Hollman, for his part, jumped at the chance to coach the Little Giants. "To me, it was probably one of the top high school programs in the state," he said. "There was a strong tradition. People had gotten used to winning." Hollman was also impressed with the strength of the support for the program. He said there was a strong junior high program and that the team had a great equipment manager in Joe Lotycz, as well as athletic trainers—commonplace now but almost unheard of in the 1970s.

Hollman was hired, and he brought with him two assistants who would succeed him as head coach: Wayne "Pete" Moore and Rex Radeloff, an Eastwood graduate who was one of Hollman's football teammates at Ohio Northern. Radeloff said the team's defensive schemes changed as the new staff took over, but the offense remained similar—a testament, Radeloff said, to the program Shuff established and left them to build on.

Hollman met the team before practice started, and Marker recalled some players viewing him as a pushover—a welcome change from Shuff's tough style. But Marker promised that within five minutes in Hollman's first practice, the players would know who's boss. "It took him four [minutes], and he was ripping them new rear ends," Marker said.

Sandusky was also in the market for a new head coach, and Gene Kidwell was succeeded by Jim Colwell. Kidwell said he enjoyed coaching but that he wanted to move into administration, and saw the opportunity that year.

The Little Giants dueled Admiral King to a scoreless tie in the Buckeye Conference opener but blew through the rest of the league, beating Findlay in Week Nine, 12–7, to clinch at least a share of its seventh Buckeye Conference title. With a win over Sandusky, Ross would have its first unbeaten season since 1957.

The Sandusky game belonged to Harry and Larry Liggins, Tommie's younger twin brothers, who would be recognized all-Ohio. Harry ran for a score and threw a pass for another, and Larry Liggins caught two touchdown passes and ran an interception back for another score. Ross won 33–0. The Ross defense, under coordinator Moore, pitched a shutout, setting a school record

Harry Liggins. *Photo courtesy of the Liggins family.*

109

Students hold up a banner celebrating Ross's undefeated season in 1974. *Photo courtesy Rutherford B. Hayes Presidential Center.*

with only thirty-three points allowed in a season. Hollman called off the dogs around halftime and started rotating in as many players as he could. Some fans, remembering the blowouts of the 1960s, wanted to see Hollman run up the score. "We could have beaten them a lot worse than we did," Hollman said. "They told me I was too kind."

The Little Giants finished 9–0–1, their fourth year in a row with nine wins. Lorain Admiral King had kept Ross from 10–0 seasons in two of those years, with a scoreless tie in 1974 and a 19–14 win in 1972. "The thorn in our side at that time was Admiral King," Radeloff said. "They always played us tough, and it seemed like they always went downhill after we played them." Ross finished the season eighth in the UPI and AP polls but once again didn't make the playoffs, despite setting program marks for yards allowed per game (113.9) and per play (2.5) on defense. "When they only took one team per region, that was tough," Radeloff said. "You had to schedule right, your opponents had to win and everything had to fall into place." Hollman was recognized as coach of the year in the league.

Once again, the Little Giants lost to Findlay in 1975, snapping a thirteen-game unbeaten streak in the Buckeye Conference. But a win at Sandusky could salvage a conference title. Mike McGilton scored for Ross, but the Little Giants missed an extra point and lost 7–6. Ross finished 6–3–1, with the three losses—to Cincinnati Elder, Findlay and Sandusky—coming by a total of sixteen points. "It was awful close to being a great season," Hollman said. "We didn't have a season to be ashamed of, but we didn't go undefeated or win the conference championship, so we viewed it as a disappointment."

The Sandusky game turned out to be Hollman's last game as Ross head coach. Hollman moved on to Wooster College, and his defensive coordinator,

The Liggins boys are recognized with their parents on Parents' Night. *Photo courtesy of the Liggins family.*

Pete Moore, became the Ross head coach. In two years as head coach, Hollman had gone 15–3–2. Moore, serving as defensive coordinator in both those years, had led a defensive unit that had shut out its opponent in eleven games and had given up a total of eighty-nine points in the other nine.

Ross was 6–1–2 going into the matchup against Sandusky in 1976, having just tied Findlay 7–7. Senior Terry Bates ran for 136 yards on thirty-three carries, including an 11-yard touchdown run in the third quarter, to bring his season total to 1,628 yards—30 more than the school record set by Jim Tiller in 1956. "Records are made to be broken, and I will be the first one to congratulate Terry for doing it," Tiller said. Rick Kusmer and Sam Davis also scored touchdowns for Ross, and Chris Myer kicked the first field goal for the Little Giants in eight years, as Ross beat Sandusky 24–3. Meanwhile, Lorain scored thirteen points—all by quarterback Steve Popovich—which was enough for a 13–8 win over Elyria, which had beaten Ross earlier in the season. Ross got the help it needed to win its fourth Buckeye Conference title in five years. Moore was named the league coach of the year.

Former Ross players Rob Lytle and Bob Brudzinski were also recognized after the 1976 season. Lytle had gone on to play running back for the University of Michigan, where he set a record with 3,307 rushing yards. He was a

Left: After graduating from Ross High School, Rob Lytle went on to an illustrious career as a running back at the University of Michigan. He was named an all-American and finished third in Heisman Trophy voting. He went on to play for the Denver Broncos. *Photo courtesy University of Michigan.*

Below: After graduating from Ross High School, Bob Brudzinski went on to an all-American career at Ohio State. He played in the NFL for the Miami Dolphins and Los Angeles Rams. *Photo courtesy Ohio State University Sports Information.*

consensus all-American and finished third in Heisman Trophy voting behind winner Tony Dorsett of Pitt and Ricky Bell of the University of Southern California. Brudzinski went to Ohio State, where he was named all-American as a defensive end (ironically, his roommate, Bob Gentry, was a football player at Sandusky). Both men were taken in the 1977 NFL draft, Brudzinski by the Rams at twenty-three, and Lytle by the Broncos at forty-five.

Gene Kidwell said that any time a Buckeye Conference player—regardless of what team he played for—succeeded, he felt like he had succeeded as well. "Those of us who felt like we prepared him on the other side of the field, we felt some ownership," he said. "Of course, that was after they graduated."

The year 1977 was a down one for the Little Giants. Ross rolled out to a 4–1 record at the midpoint of the season, with only a non-league loss to Cincinnati LaSalle, but dropped four league games to Elyria, Lorain, Marion Harding and Findlay. The four-game skid was the longest for Ross since 1969. The Little Giants got a boost midway through the season from Chuck Tiller, who transferred from Sandusky to Ross during the football season—and played for the Little Giants. Going into the Sandusky game, he was called a traitor. He ran for 97 yards and a touchdown. Senior Jeff Brown succeeded Bates at tailback. There was a drop-off in size, but Brown made up for it with speed, having been timed at 4.4 seconds in the 40-yard dash. He gained 67 yards in the game, a 14–0 Ross win, to finish the season with 1,349 yards rushing. Sandusky finished the season 8–2, good enough to win its first Buckeye Conference title since 1970, but the loss to Ross effectively kept the Blue Streaks out of the playoffs.

Super Bowl XII in January 1978 marked the first appearance by a Little Giant. That year, the Broncos met the Cowboys at the Louisiana Superdome, matching up a pair of rookie running backs: Lytle for Denver, and Dorsett for Dallas. Lytle scored the Broncos' only touchdown in the 27–10 loss. Footage from the game of Lytle running would be used in the movie *Everybody's All-American*.

In 1978, T.J. Brudzinski saw his primary offensive position go from quarterback to split end, making way for gunslinger Tom Woleslagel. The Little Giants went 5–0, with wins over Euclid, Toledo Central Catholic, Toledo St. John, Lorain Admiral King and Mansfield Senior, but lost their next four, including shutouts to Lorain, Marion Harding and Findlay. Ross was without the services of Woleslagel in the Week Nine game against Findlay, a 20–0 loss, but he had recovered suitably from the chicken pox to dress against Sandusky in Week Ten. With the Blue Streaks leading 7–0 thanks to a Kelvin Lindsey touchdown, quarterback Adam Caskey lost a fumble, which was recovered by Joe Roesch and returned 27 yards to the end zone. On the ensuing series, the Little Giants fumbled again, this time by Greg Brown, and Brian McPhillamy recovered it.

Six plays later, Lindsey ran off the left tackle and went 31 yards untouched to score. He scored twice more, rushing for 286 yards as the Blue Streaks routed Ross 34–16 to win its second consecutive Buckeye Conference title. The Little Giants' two scores came with Ross trailing 27–0 in the fourth, when Moore put Woleslagel in at quarterback. The junior responded with two touchdown passes, both to T.J. Brudzinski. All told, Woleslagel set a school record with 1,298 yards passing that year, giving some optimism to Ross fans for his senior season.

The win propelled the 9–1 Blue Streaks into the state playoffs for the first time, where they met Cincinnati Princeton at Dayton's Welcome Stadium. The Vikings prevailed 13–11 and then, on the same field a week later, beat Berea 12–10 to cap off an undefeated season with a Class AAA state championship.

The 1979 season was the first time Fremont Ross played football on artificial turf, meeting Toledo Central Catholic at the Glass Bowl, the University of Toledo's home field. In the *News-Messenger*'s annual football preview, Pete Moore put to rest a rumor, saying that the Little Giants would not need to buy special shoes to play on the turf. Ross blanked the Irish 21–0. After winning the first five games of the season, the Little Giants suffered back-to-back losses, to Elyria (3–0, on an Aaron Swann field goal) and Lorain Senior, 18–16. Ross got back on track to beat Marion Harding and shut out Findlay (its third shutout of the season) going into the grudge match against the Blue Streaks. In that game, Tom Woleslagel threw a five-yard pass to Adam Caskey to put Ross on the board, 6–0. But the Blue Streaks answered back with two scores, thoroughly dominating the game after that. With 1:01 left to play, Woleslagel found Mark Johnson for a forty-eight-yard touchdown pass. Greg Brown swept in the two-point conversion to tie the game.

The 1970s would end with a 14–14 tie between Ross and Sandusky, but it might have been the most successful decade in Fremont Ross history. The Little Giants went 71–23–6, including going 45–20–4 in the Buckeye Conference, and won four league titles, including three in a row from 1972 to 1974. In addition to Lytle, Brudzinski and Tommie Liggins, Terry Bates, Jeff Brown and David Liggins went on to play college football, at Ball State, Iowa and Arizona State, respectively. And the Little Giants had gone 6–3–1 against Sandusky—including four in a row from 1971 to 1974, the first four-game win streak for Ross since 1949—after going just 2–8 the previous decade. Radeloff recalled going with Moore to a coaches' clinic in the Cleveland area at which the special guest was Browns player Thom Darden, a 1968 Sandusky graduate. Moore and Radeloff were wearing Fremont Ross jackets, which Darden noticed and said, "We used to kick your ass."

"Come to a game now," Radeloff said. "That doesn't happen anymore."

CHAPTER 9

THE 1980s

ROSS AND SANDUSKY GO THEIR SEPARATE WAYS

In 1980, Fremont Ross got another lesson in the cruelty of the new OHSAA playoff system. The Little Giants and Blue Streaks were both 8–1 going into the season finale. Ross's lone loss that year had come to Cleveland Benedictine.

Ross thoroughly outplayed Sandusky, with junior Tony Gant pulling in three interceptions for the Little Giants. In the second quarter, Mike Eicher, who had taken over as quarterback after Tom Woleslagel's graduation, got a forty-three-yard gain on first and twenty-two from Ross's forty-eight yard line, setting the Little Giants up with first and goal from the nine. Two plays later, Eric Bates scored from six yards out, and Greg Bobay kicked the extra point. It was the game's only score, as Ross went on to win 7–0. The Little Giants won the Buckeye League title with a 9–1 record—its fifth Buckeye Conference crown since 1972 but first since 1976. The team finished the season twelfth in the UPI rankings and fifteenth in the AP poll but watched Sandusky go to the playoffs with an 8–2 record, based on computer points that decided playoff berths. It was so close that initial Associated Press reports indicated that Ross had qualified for the first time for the playoffs. "They were tied, and I think the third-level points beat them," Bob Marker said. "People were ready to go to the playoffs." The postseason had expanded that year from three to five divisions (no longer classes), and the top two teams from each region made the playoffs, making the playoffs three weeks instead of two. The Blue Streaks went on to lose 42–6 to Upper Arlington in their playoff opener.

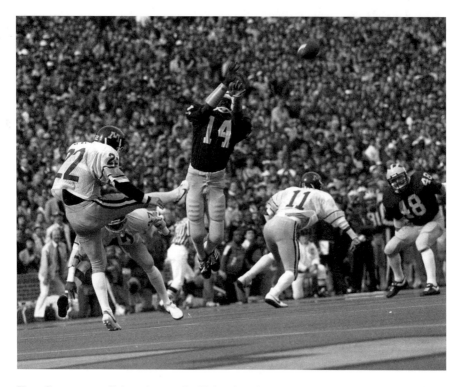

Tony Gant was an all-American at the University of Michigan after graduating from Ross. *Photo courtesy University of Michigan.*

"It was frustrating," Dick Sherman said. "There were teams we had beaten, and they beat someone else, and they'd get the points and get in."

The Little Giants made it six league titles since 1972 with a 24–8 win over the Blue Streaks in 1981. Sandusky was 8–1 going into the season finale, and Ross was 7–2, but the Little Giants held Sandusky to 56 yards rushing and 110 yards passing—and forced three Blue Streak turnovers. Meanwhile, Tony Gant, who would be named Back of the Year in Ohio, ran for three touchdowns. Gant would go on to play football at the University of Michigan. Despite the loss (Sandusky scored late to avoid the shutout), the Blue Streaks shared the Buckeye Conference title with Ross, which ended the year ranked seventeenth in UPI and AP polls and won the Toledo Blade big-school poll championship. But once again, the playoffs started without Ross.

Chuck Lindsey was back on the sidelines for Ross as a varsity assistant for Pete Moore. After graduating from Bowling Green State University in 1976, Lindsey had returned to his alma mater and had become a volunteer coach. Lindsey was the defensive backs coach and was thrilled to find that Gant, whom he called the best high school football player in the United States, was his starting free safety. "He was very coachable," Lindsey said. "He was a great student and a great kid."

The year 1982 was a disappointing one for Ross, as the Little Giants rolled into the season finale with a 3–6 record. For the first time since the infamous 1966 whitewashing, Sandusky shut out Ross, 22–0. The Blue Streaks got on the board first, in the second quarter, when Alan Antel booted a 28-yard field goal. Running back Willie Clark scored on a 16-yard touchdown run to give the Blue Streaks a 10–0 lead late in the second quarter. The Little Giants appeared to be putting a drive together, but David Turner intercepted Kevin Wilhelm, who had replaced Brian Borden as quarterback midway through the season, at the goal line and ran it to the 35. On Ross's next possession, Wilhelm fumbled, and Irwin Owens took the loose ball to the Ross 21 for the Blue Streaks, who scored six plays later when Bret Ninke hit Joe Young in the end zone. Tracy Steele scored on the next possession for Sandusky, making it 22–0. Wilhelm had thrown three interceptions, and the Little Giants could manage just seven first downs on 116 yards of total offense.

The Blue Streaks won the Buckeye Conference for the second year in a row and advanced to the playoffs but lost their opener 29–7 to Massillon. The Little Giants finished 3–7, their worst record since the 1969 team that went 2–7–1.

But today's goats are tomorrow's heroes. The 1983 Little Giants squad returned about twenty-five lettermen, and Ross was 8–0–1 (having tied Toledo St. Francis 7–7 in Week Three) going into the matchup at Strobel Field. Sandusky, at 9–0, was virtually assured of a playoff spot, if not a home game. Ross was second in the region, and the top two teams got into the playoffs. The Little Giants had to win to get in.

"We knew going into it that it was going to be a defensive battle," Radeloff said. "Both teams had great defenses, and we knew it would come down to a mistake here or there."

Kevin Wilhelm engineered a drive to give Ross a 7–0 lead with a Shawn McCarthy extra point in the first quarter, and the Little Giants defense held up, thanks in no small part to the field position game by McCarthy, also the Little Giants' punter. McCarthy would go on to play football at Purdue and kick in the NFL for the New England Patriots. Ross held on for the 7–0 win despite being outgained by Sandusky 160–133. The Little Giants finished the season third in the AP and UPI polls, but would the playoffs beckon for the first time for Ross? Would the Little Giants have to go on the road? Who would they play?

As it turns out, Harmon Field would host a rematch of the Week Ten game between Ross and Sandusky. A temporary press box was erected, and portable bleachers were set up all the way around the playing field. Bob Marker recalled going out to the field at 8:00 a.m. the Saturday of the game to find custodian Joe Lotycz and a team of workers scraping off the yard lines with shovels after a massive ice storm hit.

Demand for tickets was so great that they were sold at the Sandusky County Fairgrounds. "I'd swear there were ten thousand people there," Marker said. "Probably could have been two or three thousand more, but everyone was bundled up so much. It was freezing."

"I've never seen so many people in my life," Lindsey said. "Everyone was there." The game was scoreless until the fourth quarter, when the Little Giants engineered a fourteen-play, sixty-one-yard drive that included three third-down conversions. Todd Beatty, who led the Little Giants with fifty-one yards on fifteen carries, ran in from two yards out.

It was all the scoring the game would have, as the Little Giants held on to once again beat Sandusky 7–0. "We didn't think we'd play anyone that good," Lindsey said. "And then we ran into Princeton." Ross and its fans would travel to Dayton to face Cincinnati Princeton at Welcome Stadium in a state semifinal game. The game was almost anticlimactic for the Little Giants. They had vanquished—shut out, even—the Blue Streaks twice in one season. It was almost as sweet as a state title. Radeloff said the players weren't as emotionally stoked for Princeton, which had beaten defending state champs Archbishop Moeller, as they were for Sandusky, but that probably didn't contribute much to the 35–7 beating. "Princeton was just an awesome team," Radeloff said. Early in the game, Radeloff, who was coaching from the press box, heard from Moore on the sideline. "Do they look as good up there as they do down here?" Moore asked. The Vikings would go on to win their second state title by beating Akron Garfield 24–6 at the Horseshoe in Columbus. The Little Giants finished the season 10–1–1, matching the program record for wins in a season, and finished third in both the AP and UPI polls.

For the third meeting in a row, Ross pitched a shutout against Sandusky in 1984. Chris Simmons, who Lindsey called the best Ross athlete not in the school's hall of fame, ran for two touchdowns and 129 yards on twenty-four carries, and Shawn McCarthy booted a pair of extra points in a 14–0 win. Ross finished the season 8–2, seventeenth in the AP and UPI polls, and won another Buckeye Conference Championship. One of the Little Giants' wins was against Toledo St. Francis, 14–13, in Week Three. But the Knights wouldn't lose another game all season, culminating with a Division I state championship win over North Canton Hoover.

That year, Sandusky had a new coach—the first hire from outside the program since the Blue Streaks lured Earle Bruce away from Salem in 1960. Larry Cook was a Toledo Libbey graduate who played for Doyt Perry at Bowling Green State University, where he was part of two Mid-American Conference champion teams. In the fall of 1964, Cook became part of the coaching staff at Willard, where he ascended to the top spot in 1968. He had heard about the reputation of the Sandusky teams of the Sensational '60s, and he wanted to be a part. "I said, 'If that Sandusky job comes open, I'll apply for it," Cook said. "I always knew it was a good job." He spent twelve years at Circleville, south of Columbus, and applied for the Sandusky job in 1984, when the program was looking to go in a different direction. The cupboard was bare for Cook's first season in 1984, with only four returning letterman, all special teams players. The Blue Streaks finished 4–6 that year.

McCarthy would get the Little Giants on the board in the 1985 matchup as well, kicking a thirty-nine-yard field goal. Ross held Sandusky scoreless in that first quarter, making it thirteen straight quarters without letting Sandusky score. The Blue Streaks were held to a safety in the second quarter when McCarthy was tackled in the end zone, and a pick-six by Keith Pace. Otherwise, it was the fourth straight meeting without an offensive score for Sandusky. Meanwhile, the Little Giants got two points of their own when the Sandusky punter ran out of the end zone to pull them within three points, 8–5, but the Blue Streaks were leading until a Jim Carroll touchdown with 4:56 left in the game. Carroll added another touchdown with 1:20 left to ice the game as the Little Giants won 19–8. The win gave Ross the Buckeye Conference co-championship with Lorain Admiral King, with identical 8–2 records and 5–1 in the league. Once again, the Little Giants missed the playoffs, which had expanded to allow the top four teams in each region—a total of eighty teams throughout the state—to play in the postseason. Sandusky finished 2–8 that year, leading Cook to start fretting about his job.

That win over Sandusky in 1985 was Moore's last as Ross coach. He resigned in December, with Radeloff, who had turned down other jobs to remain an assistant at Ross, succeeding him. "It was one of those situations where he felt it was time to move on," Radeloff said. "Everyone was disappointed. Even though I got the head coaching job, I would have been happy to stay as his offensive coordinator."

Moore would go on to coach at Lima Shawnee before returning to the area to coach at Port Clinton—with Rob Lytle as one of his assistants. Moore

Derek Isaman. *Photo courtesy Ohio State University Sports Information.*

died in 2001 following a stroke at the age of fifty-five. Lindsey described Moore as a player's coach but one who was extremely loyal to his assistants. "He let his coaches coach," Lindsey said. "If he hired you, he'd defend you no matter what."

The Buckeye Conference had also started to wobble, as Lorain, Admiral King and Elyria pulled out of the league to form a new league in the Lorain County area. They were not unhappy with the Buckeye Conference, which was respected throughout the state, but felt forced to leave because of financial concerns. Lorain's identity in particular had been tied up with the steel industry, and as it started its decline in the United States in the 1970s and '80s, school districts and municipalities—particularly in Pennsylvania and Ohio—started to feel the pinch. "Take away the almighty dollar, and we would still have it," Lorain athletic director Fred Churchill said in 1986 of the Buckeye Conference. Dick Sherman, who retired in 1987 as Ross athletic director, said travel started to take its toll on the league, particularly for the schools in Lorain County. "They started looking closer to home," he said. "Mansfield started looking closer to home."

By 1986, Ross had won the previous three league titles, so players and coaches knew they would get everyone's best shot in an effort to win the league's last title. The title, as in so many other years, came down to the Sandusky-Ross game. The Little Giants and Blue Streaks each had one loss in the league when they met at Harmon Field. The game began with a Ross penalty because the pregame festivities ran long. "Everything that could go wrong in the first half did," said John Cahill, who was a senior playing in his last regular-season game. By then, Ross players saw beating Sandusky as almost a right, Cahill said, as the Little Giants had consistently beaten the Blue Streaks since he was in junior high school. A Ross win would give the Little Giants the league title and mostly likely a playoff berth in Radeloff's first year as head coach.

Charlie McGowan kicked a 23-yard field goal to put Sandusky on the board in the first, and Paul Smoot scored two touchdowns for the Blue Streaks as part of a twenty-carry night in which he gained 105 yards. McGowan missed the first point after but made the second, and Sandusky went into the locker room with a 16–0 lead. "At halftime, I was crossing my fingers that we could hold on, because they were bigger and stronger than we were," Cook said. Steve Letzring blocked a punt in the third quarter and then ran for a five-yard touchdown for Ross's first offensive points of the night, with 8:40 left in the game. John Stierwalt's extra point made it 16–9. Overall, Letzring led all rushers with 119 yards on twenty-four carries. With 1:17 left, Cahill hauled in a

The 1986 Sandusky High School football team, winners of the last Buckeye Conference title. *Photo courtesy Tom Sharrah.*

13-yard pass from Stierwalt and scored, setting up a potential game-tying extra point. It seemed like a slam dunk to Cahill, who was the holder, as Ross hadn't missed an extra point all year. But Keith Aaron, all of five feet, six inches and 145 pounds, blew through the line and blocked the extra point, giving the win to Sandusky, 16–15. The Blue Streaks finished the season tied in the league with Lorain Admiral King at 5–1. (The Admirals were 8–2 overall; Sandusky, 7–3). Ross was a game behind, finishing the season 6–4 and 4–2 in the Buckeye Conference, which had hosted its last game.

"It still makes me mad today," said Cahill, who has gone on to become a successful girls' basketball coach at Clyde High School. "They won the game fair and square, but it's one of those things I still haven't quite gotten over."

Cook realized the win over Ross probably saved his job and that it represented a turning point for the Sandusky High School program. "If

I had to point to one game that etched me as Sandusky coach in a lot of people's eyes, that was it," he said.

In June 1987, the league, which Bo Schembechler called the strongest high school conference in America, disbanded. It was (and remains) cause for mourning for those who played and coached in the league. "The Buckeye Conference was tough and athletic," Lindsey recalled. "You got your ass beat every Friday. You had to coach; you couldn't just win on talent."

Ross had had its days in the league, winning or sharing a total of thirteen championships, including three consecutive league crowns on three separate occasions: 1955–57, 1972–74 and 1983–85. The Little Giants ended the league dominating it, winning five out of its last seven championships.

But the Blue Streaks also had their share of days at the top, winning the first crown in 1954, as well as fourteen others. Sandusky won three league titles in a row twice, from 1965 to 1967 and 1981 to 1983, and won four league crowns in a row, from 1960 to 1963.

Sandusky, along with Lorain, Admiral King and Elyria, went to the Erie Shore Conference. Cook said that move was due to the salesmanship of Gene Kidwell, who was Sandusky High School principal at the time. Ross and Findlay, without a whole lot of options, went to the Buckeye Central Conference, which had such far-afield opponents as Zanesville, Newark and Lancaster, leading Marker to nickname it the "Learjet League." "It was disappointing, to say the least," Radeloff said of the disintegration of the Buckeye Conference. "It would have been great to find a conference in the Toledo area, but that wasn't going to happen. Our other option would be to go independent, and that wouldn't be good."

Lindsey said league games reminded him of playing in college. He said it wasn't uncommon for the team to leave, stop somewhere halfway for a meal and go through a walk-through and then continue on to the game. "It was new and different," Lindsey said. "I think it was harder on the parents. It hurt attendance."

And in 1987, for the first time since World War II, the Little Giants and Blue Streaks didn't meet on the field. At that point, Findlay really began to supplant Sandusky as the Little Giants' most bitter rivals, an attitude that can still be found in some circles today.

Butch Wagner said in the 1987 Pigskin Preview that every effort was made for a Ross-Sandusky meeting, but Ross wanted a home game in Week Two,

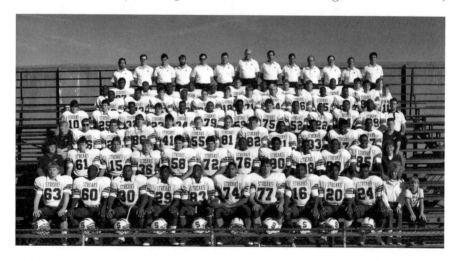

The 1988 Sandusky High School football team won its second straight Erie Shore Conference title. That year also marked the last time to date that Ross and Sandusky haven't met on the football field. *Photo courtesy Tom Sharrah.*

when Sandusky offered to meet the Little Giants. It was the Blue Streaks' turn to host, and the two teams reached an impasse. Sandusky adjusted well to life in the Erie Shore Conference, going 8–2 to win the league and winning a pair of playoff games against Logan and Brunswick before falling 21–14 in overtime to Boardman in the state semifinals. Ross got jet-lagged in the Learjet League, finishing 4–6 under Radeloff.

The Blue Streaks and Little Giants also didn't meet in 1988. Ross finished 5–5 that year, but Sandusky, with twenty-four seniors, went 9–1 to win the Erie Shore Conference and UPI poll championship and host a playoff game at Strobel Field. The Blue Streaks lost 35–21 to eventual state semifinalist Toledo Whitmer.

Lindsey said that he still hears players and coaches lamenting that Ross and Sandusky didn't meet in 1987 or 1988. "Some of the guys now say, 'We would have beat you,'" he said. "But the best team didn't always win. It was who came to play."

Sandusky's regular season ended with Vermilion. And like the pitched battles with Ross, the Vermilion game would decide the Erie Shore Conference. "It turned out to be a big rivalry game for us because it decided the league," Cook said. "But not playing Fremont…it felt like our schedule was not complete."

But Ross and Sandusky couldn't stay apart for long. The two teams would meet in the third game of the 1989 season. Ross was 1–1 going into the matchup, as Terry Carter ran all over the Blue Streaks. He had passed Rob Lytle to become the third leading rusher in Ross history the week before in a 34–16 win over Toledo Macomber, and he ran for 198 yards against the Blue Streaks to pass John "Big Thunder" Lewis for second all-time. And Ross needed every one of those yards, as Sandusky jumped out to a 17–0 lead in the first half. Scott Mezinger pulled in a tipped pass for a 62-yard touchdown to put the Little Giants on the board. Carter scored two more touchdowns (the last one with less than a minute left) as the Little Giants clawed back for a 21–17 win. Ross went on to shut out Toledo Whitmer the following week and roared through the Buckeye Central Conference, including an 18–13 comeback win against Lancaster, to win the league with an undefeated 4–0 mark. Overall, Ross finished 8–2, second in the region for computer points (guaranteeing a playoff spot) and eleventh in the Associated Press poll. By then, the AP poll was all that was left, as United Press International, the news service that served mostly afternoon newspapers, started to diminish in size and stature, eventually falling into bankruptcy. The Little Giants played Lancaster in the playoff opener and couldn't beat them twice in one year, falling 42–7. Sandusky went 8–2 to win the Erie Shore Conference.

In 1990, Ross and Sandusky again met in Week Three. The Blue Streaks had just ten seniors, and Cook felt that a 7–3 record would be a good year. Sandusky took the opening kickoff 76 yards on an eleven-play drive and scored, and that was just the start. The Blue Streaks ran for 264 yards, including 113 by Joe Matthews. Sandusky held the Little Giants to 36 yards in the first half and a total of 133 yards in the game as the Blue Streaks handed Ross its first loss of the season, 31–0. It was one of five shutouts Sandusky would have that season. "It was a game where we knew we had to play our best," Radeloff said. "They played a great game, and to be honest with you, they were probably that much better than we were."

Cook had never been a fan of having the Ross game at any point other than the last game of the season, because it took on a winner-take-all sheen, and an early loss in the rivalry game could wreck the season. On the other hand, an early win could be just the confidence builder the Blue Streaks needed. "We were able to dominate the game, and that generated a tremendous amount of confidence," Cook said. "We felt we could beat anyone."

The Blue Streaks went undefeated that year, their first 10–0 season since 1982, and advanced to the playoffs, beating Toledo St. John's 21–15 in overtime and Massillon 27–7 in the regional finals before losing 27–14 in the state semifinals to eventual state champion Warren Harding. That Harding team, which featured future Buckeye and Minnesota Viking Korey Stringer, was the first after the school consolidated with Warren Western Reserve. But even with that loss, it was still the best year in Sandusky High School history, as the Blue Streaks finished 12–1.

After losing to the Blue Streaks, the Little Giants then lost their next two, to Whitmer and Madison, before getting back in the win column with a 42–21 victory over Newark. Ross finished the season 6–4 but was tied with Lancaster with a 4–0 conference record and shared the league title, the last for the Buckeye Central Conference. In the league's four years, Ross had won two titles.

CHAPTER 10

Together Again

The Buckeye Central Conference disintegrated in 1991. Travel costs and time allotments were too much for Ross to continue in the circuit. The Little Giants turned to the Great Lakes League, a nearby league that dated back to the waning days of World War II, when it was formed as the Great Northern Conference. The league included at one point or another most large high schools around Toledo, and when Ross joined, it consisted of Fostoria, Whitmer, Bedford (Michigan), Oregon Clay, Sylvania Northview and Napoleon. The league was looking for an eighth team.

Once again, Ross and Sandusky met in Week Three. The Little Giants took a 6–0 lead and held Sandusky to a total of 181 yards of offense. Of those, 55 came on one play, a David Rogers reception off Chris Keys. Stiner Wright's extra point gave Sandusky a 7–6 lead. It was the first offensive score of the season for the Blue Streaks, and it held up, as Sandusky won by that score on its way to a 7–3 season and fourth straight Erie Shore Conference title. Sandusky coach Larry Cook said a 3–0 overtime loss in the season opener to Cleveland Benedictine kept the Blue Streaks from making their fourth trip to the playoffs in five years.

The Little Giants dropped to 1–4 with losses to Whitmer and Findlay but won their next four games, setting up a Week Ten showdown with undefeated Fostoria. A Ross win would give them a share of the Great Lakes League title. The Little Giants held the Redmen, coached by Dick Kidwell and quarterbacked by his son Derek, to fourteen points but lost 14–6. Fostoria would go on to win a Division II state title, and Derek Kidwell was named Mr. Football.

In 1992, Radeloff made Chuck Lindsey the Ross defensive coordinator, and Pete Moore rejoined the staff as an assistant. "I was happy to have him back," Radeloff said of his old friend Moore. But the biggest addition to the Ross football team was a sophomore who made a big splash early on and would continue to do great things for years to come. Charles Woodson's play had been anticipated since he was in seventh grade. He was literally born to play Fremont Ross football, with half-brothers Terry Carter and Shawn Simms both distinguishing themselves on the gridiron for the Little Giants.

Woodson played baseball with Bob Marker's son Jared, and Marker recalled meeting Woodson for the first time when he was ten years old. Woodson brashly said, "I'm going to be the best football player Ross had. I'm going to be Mr. Football, I'm going to Michigan, and I'll win the Heisman Trophy." And he accomplished every one of those goals.

"A lot of people called him cocky," Marker said. "But I think he was supremely confident in his abilities."

Radeloff told Woodson's mother that Woodson was good enough to play as a freshman, and in fact, he wanted him to do so. But his mother didn't want him playing varsity as a freshman. "I understood that, even though I wished I had him as a freshman," Radeloff said. Woodson was one of many players Lindsey saw with talent in junior high school, but Lindsey knew from firsthand experience that talent only went so far. Lindsey recognized that his playing career was based more on talent than work ethic, and he realized that he might have left some opportunities on the table—and he didn't want to see that happen with Woodson. "If I ever had a kid like that, I'm going to make sure he's ready to play," he said. "I want him to make everyone around him better."

Sandusky, on the other hand, also had a player who was making a name, not as a flashy ball carrier like Woodson, but as a lineman. Junior Orlando Pace was stunning fans, coaches and scouts with his rare mix of size and speed. "Orlando has all the tools to become a major college prospect, and he still has another year with us," Cook told the *Register*. "He's getting better and better and often takes things in his own hands. We must have an excellent year from him if we are going to be successful."

Cook recalled walking through the gym in Jackson Junior High School in Sandusky, where Pace was in eighth grade. Even at that age, he towered over everyone. "He had to be six-two," Cook said. "That caught my eye, so I watched. He moved with such agility. I went home and told my wife, 'He's going to be an all-American.'"

Marker recalled Radeloff outlining the game plan against Pace on defense, saying, "We'll run right at him." In a way, that was a mark of respect for Pace, Marker said. They didn't run away from Pace, recognizing his tremendous lateral speed. "It was amazing how big he was and how he could run," Radeloff said. "He'd run you down." Lindsey said Pace was double-teamed, with a wingback in motion coming in to help out the tackle opposite him.

Woodson had a fumble recovery for a touchdown and a receiving touchdown in the Little Giants' Week Two win over St. John's and proved it was no fluke with an 85-yard pick-six against Sandusky the following week, one of six interceptions by Woodson as a sophomore. Tyrone "Toddy" Price scored from two yards out to make it 21–14, but the Little Giants got no closer. Tron Lofton ran for three touchdowns as the Blue Streak ground-and-pound offense, with Pace throwing blocks, picked up 352 yards, including 204 rushing by Lofton. The Blue Streaks won 35–14, their third victory in a row over Ross, and would finish the year 7–3 with a loss to Vermilion to end their four-year run as ESC champions. The Little Giants finished the year 6-4. But Woodson, who was an explosive scoring threat on offense, defense and special teams, had established himself. "Anyway that was possible, he could score," Radeloff said. "There was no doubt he was going to be a great player."

Pace was featured on the cover of the *Register*'s football preview for his senior season in 1993 and was celebrated as big and quick. "Orlando's talent is unlimited, not just because he is big, but he has quick feet and agility and you rarely find that in a young man as big as he is," Cook said in the preview.

Woodson, a junior, was the featured offensive back for Ross in 1993. He was also a featured kickoff and punt returner and played defensive back as well. So the Sandusky game plan was to contain him, and it worked. Woodson gained only 68 yards on nineteen carries, but the defense's focus on him freed up quarterback Shane Moran, who went twelve-of-fourteen passing for 167 yards, including a game-winning touchdown pass to Kris Kayden with five minutes left in the game. Jason Lather also ran for a touchdown for the Little Giants, who won 20–14. For Sandusky, LeAndre Moore ran for 151 yards on fifteen carries, and Torrez Rollison had 86 yards on twenty carries. The Blue Streaks had failed to win in their first three games—with each loss by six points. It was their worst start since 1957, when they went 1–8.

Ross went 9–1 and ended the season ranked eighth in the state AP poll. It finished second in the league to Fostoria, which went undefeated again,

After graduating from Sandusky High School, all-American Orlando Pace would have a distinguished career at Ohio State, winning two Lombardi Trophies and an Outland Trophy. He was the top draft pick in the 1997 NFL draft and played twelve years for the Rams and one for the Bears. *Photo courtesy Ohio State University Sports Information.*

beating Ross 7–6, with a blocked extra point making the difference. The Little Giants also had a potential game-winning field goal blocked, too. That year, Woodson, who scored six touchdowns in a game twice, was named Offensive Back of the Year for the Great Lakes League and for the Northwest District, having ran for 1,528 yards and scored a total of twenty-seven touchdowns. By the time Woodson graduated, he would own the Ross record book.

Sandusky, meanwhile, got back on track in the Erie Shore Conference, going undefeated in the league, including a 33–13 drubbing of Vermilion in the season finale to win its fifth league title in six years and finish 7–3. Pace was named defensive player of the year in the league and first team on both sides of the ball. He was named AP district lineman of the year, while Woodson was named offensive player of the year. Pace and Woodson were also named first team all-Ohio. And Woodson would be back with the Little Giants for another year.

Pace went on to Ohio State. Cook recalled talking with Lee Owens, the Massillon coach he and the Blue Streaks beat in the 1990 playoffs. Owens, by then an Ohio State assistant, asked how good Pace was. "I said, 'When Orlando Pace gets on campus, he'll start, and he'll be a better tackle than Korey Stringer.' Lee asked me what I was smoking," laughed Cook. But as it turned out, he was right. Pace won two Lombardi Awards and the Outland Trophy. He finished fourth in the 1996 Heisman Trophy voting and was the first overall pick in the NFL draft. Cook said that was a testament not just to his "supernatural" speed and athleticism but also to his ability to take direction and his need to improve. "He was so coachable," Cook said. "He'd hang on your every word. I knew the sky was the limit for him—and it was."

Leading up to the eighty-ninth installment of Ross-Sandusky in 1994, Cook made it a point to practice special-teams play, knowing that Woodson was dangerous on kickoff and punt returns. Paco Romero punted, and the ball appeared to get to the corner of the field, near the sideline. "We worked all week long on punt coverage," Cook recalled eighteen years later, his head in his hands. "We kicked it right where we wanted to, and we couldn't put a glove on him." Woodson returned Romero's punt seventy-five yards for a score to put Ross on the board. Woodson would graduate with the school record for punt return touchdowns, which he still holds with five. Jason Lather scored on a twenty-yard run for the Little Giants in the second quarter, and Woodson would score twice more before halftime, on a thirty-yard pass from Shane Moran and a twenty-eight-yard fumble recovery. To prove he couldn't do everything, Woodson was 0-for-1 passing in the game. Moran ran for a pair of touchdowns himself, and Jeremy Lozano caught a sixty-six-yard touchdown pass from Jeremy Rakes. The Blue Streaks avoided a shutout with a ninety-yard fumble recovery by Marcel Gowdy with 1:04 left in the game, and Romero, who had indirectly initiated the scoring in the game, capped it with an extra point, as Ross won 46–7. Marker was in the Sandusky locker room after the game and heard some assistant coaches complaining that the Little Giants had run up the score, with Woodson continuing to play into the fourth quarter. One of the assistants at Sandusky at the time was Tony Munafo, who had been a Blue Streaks assistant under Earle Bruce in the 1960s before going on to coach at Huron. Marker recalled him quieting the assistants by saying, "I think these people still remember the game where we beat them 74–0." The 46–7 margin was the worst beating either team had been handed since the infamous 74–0 whitewashing in 1966. Sandusky finished the season 7–3 for its second straight ESC title—and its sixth in seven seasons. As it turned out, it would be the last title Sandusky won in the Erie Shore Conference.

Woodson would go on to break the single-game rushing record against Oregon Clay, as the Little Giants won their first Great Lakes League title, going 5–1 in the league to tie with Fostoria. The Redmen beat Ross 22–15, without Woodson, who was out with bursitis. But for the first time since 1989, the Little Giants would play in Week Eleven, facing Massillon Washington at Byers Field in Parma. Prior to the game, Sandusky coach Larry Cook addressed the Little Giants, reflecting on the Blue Streaks' win over Massillon in the 1990 playoffs and telling them not to be awed by the Tiger mystique. Woodson ran for 231 yards to finish his high school career with a school-record 3,861 yards rushing and scored four touchdowns, but it wasn't enough, as the Tigers took a 35–28 lead in the fourth quarter. The Little Giants started driving for a potential tying or winning score. At the time, high school rules didn't allow the quarterback to spike the ball to stop the clock. Radeloff wanted to call that play at several points on the final drive but couldn't, since it would have been called intentional grounding. Ross drove to the Washington two-yard line with nine seconds left, but an interception on the last play of the game sealed the Massillon win. "If I was a spectator, I would have loved that game," Radeloff said. "It

In 1997, Ross alumnus Charles Woodson would become the first and, to date, only primarily defensive player to win a Heisman Trophy. He has played in the NFL for both the Raiders and the Green Bay Packers, with whom he won a Super Bowl. *Photo courtesy University of Michigan.*

was a great game. They may have had better athletes than we did, but we had the best athlete on the field."

Woodson finished his senior season with 2,028 yards rushing and 230 points, both single-season marks. He also graduated as the career leader in scoring, with 464 points; offensive yards, with 4,636; and punt return yards, with 683. In a three-year career, Woodson had gained 5,757 all-purpose yards and scored seventy-seven touchdowns. "He was probably the best athlete I had ever seen play football," Radeloff said of Woodson. "He had a feel for the game. He could sense what was going to happen. I was fortunate he was on our side of the field."

Woodson was named offensive back of the year once again in the GLL and in the Northwest District. But despite his offensive exploits, carrying the ball wasn't where his interest was. "I love defense," he said when he was named Mr. Football by the Ohio Associated Press. "I love coming up and making the hits."

In 1995, the Little Giants were listing going into the Sandusky matchup, having been shut out by Columbus DeSales (20–0) and Akron Buchtel (19–0). It was the first time since 1931 that Ross began a season with two shutout losses. Ross scored its first touchdown of the season on a methodical drive after receiving the opening kickoff of the second half against Sandusky, getting a 10–8 lead. Harry Liggins Jr. intercepted a pass to end a Sandusky drive, and Derek Thiessen had a one-yard touchdown run, set up by a thirty-seven-yard interception return by Justin Conklin, to give Ross a 16–8 lead. But the Blue Streaks battled back to tie the game, sending it to overtime.

The era of ties in Ohio high school football was over, as each team was guaranteed at least one possession in overtime. Ross's Rakes, who had missed an extra point and a field goal earlier in the game, booted a thirty-three-yard field goal. On the ensuing possession, the Little Giants defense blocked a potential game-tying field goal to preserve the 19–16 win. Ross went on to go 6–1 in the league, losing once again to Fostoria, but shared the Great Lakes League title with the Redmen and Whitmer. Sandusky went 7–3 for the third straight year, but this time, that wasn't good enough to win the Eastern Shore Conference title.

In 1996, Ross was looking to do something it hadn't done since 1974: win four straight against Sandusky. And the Little Giants used the big plays, a Harry Liggins Jr. thirty-three-yard run and a Derek Thiessen eighty-yard run, to mount a 14–0 lead. But the momentum shifted as the first half ended, and Sandusky reeled off twenty-four points with a scoring run by Darin Williams, a twenty-five-yard field goal by Mike Poeschle and touchdown passes from

The 1995 Sandusky High School team. *Photo courtesy Tom Sharrah.*

Jeremy Newell to Marcel Gowdy and Darcel Irby to Orlando Williamson to win 24–14 and snap Ross's three-game win streak in the rivalry. That year, Ross finished 7–3, while Sandusky went 8–2.

One by one, the Little Giants were rejoined by Buckeye Conference rivals. Ross's old rival Findlay had joined the GLL in 1995 to give the league its eighth team. That only lasted a year when Northview left. In 1997, Sandusky joined the league, and once again, the Little Giants and Blue Streaks would play for a league title. "It felt right to be in the same league as Ross and to play them at the end of the year," Cook said.

The day before Ross's Week Seven matchup with Oregon Clay, Rex Radeloff announced his resignation as coach, effective at the end of the season. Radeloff, who had been associated with the Little Giants for more than twenty years, felt it was time to go. Ross, then 3–3 and coming off an 18–0 loss to Fostoria—a team on its way to its second state title—responded by winning its last four games to finish 7–3.

Radeloff's resignation (he would retire from the Fremont City Schools the following year) ended a string of succession that spanned twenty-four years, starting with Tom Hollman, who was assisted and succeeded by Pete Moore, who was then assisted and succeeded by Radeloff.

Ross looked east for its next coach, hiring Dan Pallante away from Boardman, a school in suburban Youngstown whose alumni include Bernie Kosar. Pallante, a native of nearby Canfield, had gone 22–21 in four years coaching the Spartans. His best year was 1995, when Boardman went 10–3, was a Division I final-four team and shared its conference title.

Pallante had been an assistant to Bill Bohren on the 1988 Spartans team that beat Sandusky in a regional final playoff game. Pallante recalled later that although the Blue Streaks were probably a superior team, Boardman was able to win in overtime—a win Cook attributes to a bad call by a referee on a Spartans punt. The official ruled that a Sandusky player touched the ball, giving Boardman the ball at the Sandusky three-yard line and setting up a game-tying score.

Pallante's first Sandusky game at the helm of the Little Giants was a pressure cooker in its own right. The Little Giants came out of the gate roaring in 1997, taking all comers. Ross was able to get the monkey off its back by beating defending state champion Fostoria but needed a late touchdown and a missed game-winning field goal by Findlay to remain undefeated going into the Sandusky game in Week Ten. The Blue Streaks, on the other hand, were 7–2, out of the GLL race and out of the playoff picture.

Sandusky's Cassell Causey fumbled the ball on the Blue Streaks' seventeen-yard line, and on the first play from scrimmage, Ross quarterback Aaron Coonrod hit Brett Hufford with a touchdown pass to put the Little Giants on the board. Sandusky then methodically marched down the field, taking 7:40 of the first quarter with a sixteen-play, sixty-nine-yard drive, culminating in a one-yard run by Causey. The extra point was no good, and it was as close as Sandusky got for the rest of the night. Josh Liggins and Demetris Sims would add rushing touchdowns, as the Little Giants won 21–6 to clinch their first 10–0 season since 1956 and their third Great Lakes League title in four years. It was the first unbeaten season for Ross since the 1974 squad had gone 9–0–1, in Tom Hollman's first year as Ross coach. "I knew they were going to have a good team," Radeloff said. "They had a good group of athletes coming back. And good kids, too."

But even at 10–0, Ross couldn't crack the AP top ten, only getting as high as twelfth. Pallante wasn't from the area, but he quickly understood the significance of the game. "If you're a Fremonter, you want to beat Sandusky," he said before the 1998 game. "And if you're from Sandusky, you want to beat Fremont. It's just the natural way to end the season. It means a lot to me."

Even with an undefeated season, newspaper accounts of the day were cautiously optimistic, saying the playoffs were possible. As it turned out, Ross did get into the playoffs, as the Little Giants would face Toledo St. Francis the following Saturday at Oregon Clay. The Knights put together a ten-play, eighty-yard drive to open the game and systematically shut Ross down for a 27–0 loss—Pallante's first as Little Giants head coach.

But Ross fans still had cause for celebration that fall, as Charles Woodson was awarded the Heisman Trophy. "I never realized how good he was until I saw him at the University of Michigan his junior year," Lindsey said of Woodson, who remains the only primarily defensive player to win the award, beating out Tennessee quarterback Peyton Manning. Dick Sherman spends his summers in Tennessee, and when he's asked about what he did for a living, he tells people about his time at Fremont Ross—and the athletes the school's produced. "Did you ever hear of Charles Woodson?" he'll ask. He said the reply is always some variation of, "Yes, and we still hate him." Marker said Woodson was good enough of an athlete that he could have played basketball or baseball on the collegiate level. "I've never seen a kid like him," he said. "They probably only needed one outfielder when he was out there. He could get anything."

In 1998, the Little Giants won their first seven games, putting together a seventeen-game win streak for Pallante. But Ross stumbled, losing a non-league game to Mansfield Senior and a league game to Findlay to set up a two-game skid going into the Sandusky game.

The Blue Streaks, on the other hand, were going through a snakebit year. Sandusky started the year sitting on 599 wins. But the Blue Streaks opened the season with a loss and kept on losing until a win over Oregon Clay for the 600th victory, a milestone in Ohio football history. Sandusky was gunning for number 601 against its oldest rivals, and the Blue Streaks took an early lead on the first of Aaron Williamson's two touchdown passes to El Da'Sheon Nix.

Williamson passed for 294 yards, a GLL record at the time, but made two mistakes that turned into scores for Ross: a pass intercepted for a seventy-one-yard touchdown by Coonrod, and another pick-six by Josh Liggins, Harry's son.

Coonrod rushed for 106 yards and three touchdowns and threw two passes—one an eighteen-yard touchdown strike to Josh's cousin Tyson Liggins, the second generation of Ligginses to distinguish themselves on the Ross gridiron. Jimmie Cherry ran for two scores for Sandusky, but the Little Giants rolled 49–28 to finish 8–2 and share the GLL crown with Findlay and Bedford. Ross finished ninth in its region, but the top four teams went to the playoffs at the time. Sandusky's win over Clay turned out to be the Blue Streaks' only one of the season, as they finished 1–9.

In two years, Pallante had gone 18–2 with a playoff berth and two league titles. Optimism was running high in Fremont, but Pallante had the itch to serve as an administrator, so he left Fremont to become the football coach and athletic director at Canon-McMillan High School outside of Pittsburgh. The new job would be closer to his hometown as well. He was hired in April, leaving the Little Giants scrambling for a replacement—and inadvertently setting off years of tumult and uncertainty at the helm for a program that had enjoyed remarkable success and stability for most of its existence.

CHAPTER 11

AND APART AGAIN

Ross and Sandusky had been in the same conference since 1997, when the Blue Streaks joined the Great Lakes League. In 1999, the OHSAA playoffs expanded yet again, allowing the top eight teams in each region into the postseason. To appear in a state championship game would now mean a fifteen-game season for a team.

In 1999, the Little Giants were trying to salvage a season under new coach Mike Eicher, the first Ross graduate since Legs Binkley to coach the Little Giants. A slow start in 1999 effectively killed any league or playoff hopes, but Ross had won three of its last four to come into the Sandusky showdown with a record of 4–5. The Blue Streaks were coming in the opposite direction, having charged out of the gate 4–1 and garnered statewide recognition in the Associated Press poll only to go 1–3 afterward to drop out of league and playoff contention.

The game was scoreless going into the second quarter, as Ross and Sandusky traded punts in a field-position battle. The Blue Streaks got the better of the battle, launching a sustained drive that ended with a Mark Wooten one-yard score. Juan Romero made the extra point and tacked on a field goal before halftime to give Sandusky a 10–0 lead at the break. The Little Giants were able to score on a three-yard run by Kendrid Nason with 2:51 to play. Brian McCord's extra point was blocked, and Ross kicked it away to put the game in the defense's hands. The Little Giants held Sandusky to a three-and-out and got the ball back at their twenty with 1:32 left to play.

Ross got to its forty-six-yard line but no closer, as the Little Giants turned the ball over on downs to end the game with a 10-6 Sandusky win, as the two teams got chippy in the post-game handshake. The loss clinched the Little Giants' second losing season in thirty years—and its first since 1987.

But the following year, Ross took out its frustrations on a one-win Sandusky team at Harmon Stadium, rolling out to a 14–0 lead less than four minutes into the game. Jamin Lozano returned the opening kickoff eighty-six yards for a score, and after a Ross defensive stop, Bo Martin scored on a fifty-one-yard sprint. Aaron Hines and Tommy Wagner each scored twice in the 41–0 rout. The Little Giants finished the season 6–4, a game back of Fostoria and Whitmer in the GLL race and just out of the money in the playoff hunt.

In 2001, Larry Cook stepped down as Sandusky head coach. In his sixteen years, the Blue Streaks had gone 111–69, a .620 winning percentage, with three seasons of at least ten wins. Cook had a total of four losing seasons as Blue Streaks coach (his first two, and two of his last three), and had won the last Buckeye Conference title and six Erie Shore Conference crowns. Cleveland Collinwood coach Phil Gary was tapped for the job.

Also that year, Ross coach Mike Eicher was not retained, in the wake of money management issues. The Little Giants hired assistant principal and 1970 Ross graduate Mike Wetzel to coach for a year. Wetzel wanted Eicher to stay on as an assistant, but the school board didn't approve, and Eicher ended up as an assistant coach at Fostoria. Jim Bollenbacher and Toby Notestine, two Sandusky assistants passed over in favor of Gary, joined Eicher's staff, as did former Blue Streaks assistant Ben Ohlenmacher. Cook could have joined them as well, as he was contacted about taking the Ross job. "We would have been interested in Larry coming over," Ross athletic director Art Bucci said. "It would have been a good fit." But Cook was retired and decided to stay retired. "If I wanted to coach anymore, I would have taken the job," he said.

The Great Lakes League became kind of fluid in 2001, when Bedford (Michigan) departed. That year, Ross came into the Sandusky game against new coach Phil Gary needing a win and some help to win the conference title. The defense was also playing for coordinator Chuck Lindsey, who had announced his intention to not return as an assistant coach at the beginning of the year. Lindsey, a Ross graduate, had spent twenty-five years as an assistant coach, including ten as defensive coordinator, where his pupils included Charles Woodson.

The Little Giants offered up the finest tribute they could to a defensive coordinator, pitching a shutout against the Blue Streaks and scoring twice on defense in a 21–0 win. Chad Clark scored on a quarterback sneak on a short drive started with a Trevor Dehn fumble recovery at the Sandusky 32. Bo Martin and Tommy Wagner each returned interceptions for touchdowns, of 70 and 58 yards, respectively. All told, the Little Giants gained 135 yards on offense—all on the ground—for the fourth rivalry win in five years by the Little Giants. But the Trojans held off Fostoria for a 21–20 win, as the Redmen failed on a potential game-winning two-point conversion with four ticks left. Findlay had beaten Ross earlier in the season, 21–14, to go undefeated in the league. That loss was the only conference setback for the Little Giants, who had started out 0–4 but went 4–2 after that.

Lorain Southview and Lorain Admiral King joined the league in 2002 but left before ever playing a game in it. Also in 2002, Great Lakes League charter members Oregon Clay and Toledo Whitmer left the conference for the Toledo City League, and Fostoria, another old Ross rival, left for the Northern Ohio League to be replaced by Napoleon. The GLL then added on Marion Harding (an old Buckeye Conference foe for the Blue Streaks and Little Giants) and Lima Senior, both independents at the time, and became the Greater Buckeye Conference.

That spring, the Fremont School Board hired Lindsey to serve as Ross head football coach. Jim Bollenbacher was a finalist for the job, and Tom Kiser also applied. Lindsey was an all-conference defensive back who had returned to Fremont to teach and coach at his alma mater, serving as a football assistant and head baseball coach—a job he quit when he was named head football coach.

Lindsey's first year as Ross coach was snakebit, to say the least. The Little Giants were 0–9 heading into the Sandusky game and hadn't come within three touchdowns of an opponent. Their losses included a 76–6 shellacking by Massillon Washington, a 56–0 shutout by Findlay and a 41–6 loss to Napoleon. But the Blue Streaks were demonstrating signs that they could be had by Ross, as they had a four-game losing streak of their own going into the game.

On the day before the annual meeting, the Ross freshmen routed Sandusky 58–14, led by quarterback Aaron Opelt. Opelt had never played football until junior high school, when he joined the team because his friends did. He tried out for running back and after a run threw the ball back to coach Greg Gallagher—with a little zip. "And he said, 'You're my quarterback,'" Opelt recalled.

Kyle Cook, one of Opelt's best friends, caught a touchdown reception in the freshman game, as the Little Giants tallied more than four hundred yards of total offense. The win, which clinched the GLL title for the freshman team, gave fans a glimpse of what could come.

However, the varsity team didn't fare so well the next day, losing 13–0 to Sandusky and snapping a four-game winning streak in the series. Ross gained a total of just thirty-two yards of offense, unable to get out of its half of the field. The Little Giants' fifty-five points were the fewest in a ten-game season since the 1940 squad had scored forty-six. It was Ross's first winless ten-game season and its first winless season since going 0–6–1 in 1918. Dennarius Walk scored a fifteen-yard rushing touchdown in the first quarter on a rainy night in Fremont.

Lindsey would be back in 2003 as Ross coach, and new GBC member Lima Senior provided him what turned out to be his only win as Ross head coach, a 13–7 victory two weeks before the Ross-Sandusky game. The Blue Streaks coach was now former Ross and Sandusky assistant Jim Bollenbacher.

The Blue Streaks got out to a 21–7 lead, with all three touchdowns scored by Ron Pickens. A Ross punt by Jake Kingsborough was blocked by Sandusky's Chris Pollard, and the Blue Streaks set up shop at the Little Giants' fifteen-yard line. Four plays later, Pickens scored his fourth touchdown of the game, from five yards out. On the ensuing Ross possession, Pollard intercepted Jarrod Marroquin, who started as Ross quarterback in place of Opelt, who was starting to put up big numbers but also demonstrate the brittleness that would plague him throughout high school and college. Pickens then scored his fifth touchdown of the game. After another Ross interception, this one by Rob Hall, Matt Feltner hit Trevor Dehn to make it 42–7 at the half. The Blue Streaks had scored three touchdowns in less than three minutes. Ross was able to score two touchdowns but still lost 42–21.

After the season, Lindsey wasn't renewed as Ross football coach, and the school district started looking for a new coach. "I have no bad feelings for Fremont Ross," Lindsey said. "I had an opportunity to do something, it didn't work out, and we moved on. I love Fremont Ross. I will always love Fremont Ross."

Lindsey was a hall-of-fame athlete at Ross, but the next coach would be someone familiar to Ross fans as an opponent, as Derek Kidwell was named the fourth Ross coach in five years in 2004.

After winning the Ohio Mr. Football Award for leading Fostoria to a Division II state title in 1992, Kidwell went on to Bowling Green State University. He was an assistant for his father Dick when the Redmen won another state title in 1996, and he spent time as an assistant coach at Lima Senior before getting hired as the head football coach at Hopewell-Loudon

High School in Bascom, between Fostoria and Fremont. The Chieftains fielded a football team for the first time in 1972 and had been a fair-to-middling team in the Midland Athletic League—until Kidwell took over. The Chieftains went 4–6 in his first year in 2000 and then 5–5 in his second year. The next two years, they went 8–2 and made the school's first and second playoff appearances.

Kidwell and his father, who would serve as offensive coordinator, were going to implement a spread offense–which was good news for Opelt, who would be able to throw the ball around and run to his heart's content. "They brought an offense in that let me show my strengths," Opelt said. "They gave me a lot of freedom." Kidwell, for his part, recognized Opelt's talent, saying, "I think he can be a big-time quarterback." Opelt, who was already getting college attention for his baseball skills, started thinking that playing football in college wasn't out of the realm of possibility.

Kidwell ended up being suspended for a violation of OHSAA rules, missing the Little Giants' second game of the year, a 21–14 loss to Toledo St. Francis. The Little Giants lost their first four games out of the chute on Kidwell's watch, and Ross fans started to wonder if the right decision had been made. But in Week Five, the Little Giants beat Columbus St. Charles, and the following week they upset a state-ranked Marion Harding team for Kidwell's first signature win as Ross coach. By the time the Sandusky game rolled around, the Little Giants were 4–5, and a Ross win coupled with a Findlay victory over undefeated Napoleon would give the Little Giants a share of their first Greater Buckeye Conference title and their first league crown since 1998.

It was also personal. In addition to losing the last two to Sandusky, the Blue Streaks had knocked Ross out of the basketball playoffs earlier that year.

The Trojans held up their end, beating the Wildcats 24–7 and tying for the league title. Jordan Edwards, who had transferred from Ross to Sandusky, put the Blue Streaks on the board with a sixty-nine-yard punt return. The Blue Streaks then recovered an on-side kick, called by Sandusky assistant Tom Kiser, who was one of the finalists for the Ross job when Kidwell got it. In the second quarter, Cory Bowling pulled Ross within one, but the extra point sailed left, leaving Sandusky with a 7–6 lead.

In the second half, Ron Pickens, who had torched Ross the year before, scored on a one-yard run to widen the lead to 14–6. Opelt led Ross in a no-huddle offense and drove down the field to score on a one-yard run by Anthony Brown. Opelt slipped and couldn't complete the two-point conversion.

It appeared the Little Giants held Sandusky to a three-and-out, but after stuffing Pickens, Ross got flagged for a personal foul, giving the Blue Streaks fifteen yards and new life to a drive that culminated in a forty-three-yard touchdown pass by Matt Feltner to Greg Garrett to make it a two-score game. The Little Giants couldn't get into the end zone, and Sandusky ended up winning its third game in a row, 21–12. The Little Giants finished 4–6 and 3–2 in the league, a game back.

The 2005 season got out to a good start for Ross, with road wins over Perrysburg and Toledo Central Catholic, but Ross came home to the new FieldTurf at Harmon Field and lost four in a row. In fact, Ross went winless at home all year but was undefeated on the road going into the Sandusky game at Strobel Field.

It was the 101st meeting between the two teams, all but one having come during the regular season. There were ceremonies before the game recognizing former players and coaches. Ross was 4–5, and Sandusky was 3–6. There were no league titles or playoff berths on the line. But for Aaron Opelt, it was nothing less than a matter of honor. "There was no way I was going to go out without a win against Sandusky," he said. "There was a little chip on our shoulder that year—like there always is against Sandusky."

The Blue Streaks got the ball on the opening drive and took it downfield as Edwards, the Ross transfer, scored for the Streaks. A missed extra point by Jeremy Strohm left it 6–0. Ross linebacker Aaron Hinkle picked up a Sandusky fumble and, hearing no whistle, ran it thirty-four yards to the end zone. Blair Ellenberger's extra point gave Ross the 7–6 lead.

The Little Giants exploded for twenty-one points in the second quarter, with an Aaron Opelt twenty-three-yard run for a score and two touchdown passes to Kyle Cook, one with five seconds left in the half as Ross took a 28–6 lead. Opelt and Cook would hook up once more for a score, and Opelt also threw a touchdown pass to Ryan Ottney.

Opelt and Cook were in the zone that night; they realized what was at stake. "We were clicking," Opelt said. "Kyle had the game of his life. We both knew it was our last chance to play together."

Edwards scored another touchdown, and Matt Feltner hit Terrance Churchwell on a twenty-three-yard scoring strike, but the Little Giants cruised to a 42–20 win. After the game, the Ross seniors talked about how much they appreciated the people they played with and for and that although they'd only seen ten wins in their high school careers, they wouldn't have done it any differently.

After the game, Sandusky coach Jim Bollenbacher appealed to his team's sense of history, saying, "Would any of you give up the experience? They played a hell of a football game." The win clinched the first non-losing

Ross alumnus Aaron Opelt went on to play football at the University of Toledo. *Photo courtesy University of Toledo Sports Information.*

season for Ross since 2000, but Kidwell wasn't finished yet, pulling Hinkle aside and saying, "This won't be our last game next year."

Fremont fans got to see no shortage of playoff football, as the FieldTurf installed at Harmon Field led to the facility hosting multiple playoff games. One of the teams was Avon Lake, the 2003 state champions and 2004 state runners-up. The Shoremen beat Olentangy Liberty at what was now being called Don Paul Stadium at Harmon Field, named after the car dealer whose donation enabled Ross to install turf. The following week, Avon was knocked off by Toledo Central Catholic in Fremont. The Don also hosted Patrick Henry on its way to a state title. The Irish would win the Division II state championship, and for the second time in school history, Ross handed a state champion its only loss of the year. The Little Giants had edged Toledo St. Francis 14–13 in 1984, when the Knights won the Division I state title.

In 2006, Kidwell set high expectations. It was his third year, and it was time to find out if everyone was buying into the program. The players were told there were low expectations, that the previous year's team had more talent. Opelt had graduated but before doing so had smashed all of Tom Woleslagel's passing records for Ross. Now Ryan Ottney would be quarterback. He had taken some snaps in garbage time the previous year but had caught passes from Opelt.

The Little Giants would not be denied. They had won their first nine games, and with a win over Marion Harding in Week Nine, they had clinched at least a share of the Greater Buckeye Conference. But Sandusky, which was 3–6 going into the matchup in Fremont, had a chance to play spoiler in new coach Mike Franklin's first year.

Devin Johnson, who had emerged as the Little Giants' running back, put Ross on the board with a thirty-six-yard touchdown run in a drive that was extended by an Ottney run on a fake punt. It was the first of Johnson's two touchdown runs that day. The Blue Streaks returned scoring with a forty-yard pick-six by Jonny Spearman. The extra point attempt by Spencer Farrar was blocked. This would turn out to be Sandusky's only score of the game, as Ross rolled to a 49–6 win, the largest margin of victory by the Little Giants in the rivalry. Ottney, who would graduate with multiple Ross single-season passing records, had four touchdown passes: two to Paul Hershey and one each to Terence Davis and Cory Clayton.

Ross capped off its first 10–0 season since 1997, finishing sixth in the AP poll. And for the first time since the 1983 playoff game against Sandusky, the Little Giants would host a playoff game. Canton McKinley lost to Massillon Washington, and Ross vaulted past the Bulldogs. The Little Giants got Toledo Whitmer, a team they had beaten in Week Two, and had no particular desire to meet for a rematch. It appeared Ross would beat Whitmer, as the Little Giants were driving in the fourth quarter to make it a two-score game, but the Panthers had been blitzing the corners all night and finally got through, as David Donovan caught an Ottney option pitch to Johnson on the fly and ran it back for what turned into the game-winning score in a 21–17 Panthers victory, providing another bitter end to a Fremont Ross playoff appearance.

In 2007, Fostoria St. Wendelin, a team that had made a state title game appearance in 1982 but in more recent years had struggled to even field a football team, announced its intention to move out of the Midland Athletic League in football. That set in motion a chain of events that led to the end of the Greater Buckeye Conference.

St. Wendelin's departure opened up a spot in the league's football schedule. An even number of teams in a league means that during the conference schedule, every team has a conference game. Lakota High School—small in enrollment but the largest school district in Ohio in terms of area—jumped at the chance to leave the Suburban Lakes League for the MAL.

The SLL found itself with seven teams, necessitating that one team play a non-league game during every week of the conference season. That league found itself looking for new members, and the conference broke up. Gibsonburg joined the Toledo Area Athletic Conference, while the other six teams—Elmwood, Eastwood, Woodmore, Lake, Otsego and Genoa—formed a new league, the Northern Buckeye Conference, along with Fostoria, formerly of the GLL and now of the NOL, and Rossford from the Northern Lakes League.

With those leagues looking for new schools, they turned their sights to the Greater Buckeye Conference. In terms of enrollment, Napoleon was the smallest school in the GBC, and Sandusky had dropped to Division II in 2003. Geographically speaking, Sandusky would be a good fit in the NOL, as would Napoleon in the NLL. The Greater Buckeye Conference was starting to break up.

But there were still some pitched battles to be had. In 2008, Ross trailed 10–0 at the half at Don Paul Stadium and 20–12 with 7:48 left to play. Ross covered ninety yards in seven plays and ninety seconds, with James Spencer scoring a touchdown. The kickoff to Sandusky was a high, arching boot that was fumbled by the return team—and picked up by the Little Giants' Greg Brown at the Sandusky thirty-seven-yard line. Brown then took a pitch from scrimmage from quarterback Cody Foos and ran it in for what turned out to be the winning score, as the Ross defense held on to preserve the 26–20 win. It was the fourth year in a row the Little Giants had beaten their oldest rivals.

Ross ended up 8–2—and on the outside looking in for the playoffs. The year before, Ross had capped off a 7–3 season with a 24–8 win at Sandusky. But the week before, the Little Giants lost to Napoleon and not only had to win at Strobel Field but looked for help they didn't get. In 2008, Ross finished a game better and still couldn't make it into the playoffs.

The Sandusky Blue Streaks celebrate their 30–0 win over Fremont Ross at Strobel Field in 2009. The team won a share of the Greater Buckeye Conference with the win. *Photo courtesy Sandusky Register.*

In 2009, the Ross-Sandusky game was recognized by iHigh.com and the U.S. Marine Corps as a Great American Rivalry game. Ross had started out 4–1 but limped their way through the GBC season, beating only Marion Harding before heading into the Sandusky game. The Blue Streaks, on the other hand, started out 0–3 but had recovered to go 4–2, including 3–1 in the conference. They were playing for a share of the league title—and still smarting at dropping a ten-point halftime lead the year before.

Once again, the Blue Streaks led 10–0 at the half. But this year, they wouldn't be denied, piling on another twenty points and shutting out Ross's listing offense. One Sandusky score was precipitated by the Little Giants muffing a kickoff in nearly the same fashion that the Blue Streaks did the year before, prompting Ross coach Derek Kidwell to say in a postgame interview, "Karma can be a mother."

Sandusky won 30–0. It was the first win over Ross since 2004 and the first shutout win against the Little Giants since the 0–10 season of 2002. But the humiliating loss turned out to be a motivator for Ross the following year.

As the Greater Buckeye Conference was breaking up, administrators at the league schools were looking for a new home. The prospect of going independent (along with the potential travel) brought flashbacks of the "Learjet League" of the Buckeye Central Conference and was something that didn't appeal to anyone. But at the same time, the league would have to be a good fit. Since neither the Northern Lakes League nor the Northern Ohio League seemed interested in Ross, administrators ended up looking to Toledo.

The Toledo City League was formed in 1926 and consisted of Toledo Public Schools high schools and other area schools, including Whitmer and Clay, which had abandoned the Great Lakes League, and the city's Catholic schools. Originally, Ross administrators weren't keen on applying to the City League, which had gate-sharing between the home and away teams. But as the Greater Buckeye Conference continued to sink, the City League represented a lifeboat. In Northwest Ohio, there weren't a lot of options for big schools, and although Ross was nominally Division I and was expected to drop to Division II for football, it was still one of the bigger schools in northwest Ohio. Findlay, Lima and Ross all applied for membership into the Toledo City League. Ross was accepted and would begin play in the 2011–12 school year.

Ross athletic director Art Bucci went to his first City League meeting, where league officials revealed an unfortunate turn of events. The Toledo Public Schools were facing a budget crunch, and it was going to take its toll on sports. Some sports were eliminated, and the sports that remained saw junior varsity, freshmen and junior high teams cut. Ross wasn't even a voting member in the City League at that point. "I went out to my car, I sat there for a minute and I almost cried," Bucci said. "I thought, 'What the hell are we going to do?'"

Ross could go independent, but that presented a logistical nightmare. It could stay in the City League, with non-league matchups taking the place of games and sports that got cut within the league—an option that was almost equally as distasteful. But there was a third route.

"We have to form our own league," Bucci said as he started meeting with counterparts at Toledo Whitmer and Oregon Clay.

The Oregon School Board passed a measure allowing administrators to start looking at other leagues, and Clay did apply to join the NLL before it took Napoleon.

It wasn't a new idea for larger schools in northwest Ohio that weren't part of Toledo Public Schools to form their own conference. In 1976, Whitmer—then an independent after having left the Great Lakes League—contacted other schools, including Buckeye Conference members Ross, Findlay, Marion and Sandusky, about forming a new conference of schools through northwest Ohio. And in 1981, Findlay hosted a meeting of area athletic directors. Both times, the Buckeye Conference stayed intact.

The result this time was the Three Rivers Athletic Conference, which would consist of three teams from the GBC—Ross, Findlay and Lima Senior—and the non-Toledo Public Schools in the City League: Clay, Whitmer, Central Catholic, St. John's Jesuit, St. Francis, Notre Dame and St. Ursula. The other member of the GBC, Marion Harding, would become an independent team. The last year for the GBC would be 2010.

The Little Giants put together their best year in 2010 since the undefeated season of 2006. Ross rolled over Toledo Start 17–0 in the opener and prevailed 22–16 over Whitmer in game two. The Little Giants journeyed to Frost-Kalnow Stadium in Tiffin and watched a track meet descend into a blowout, losing 40–21 to Columbian. They recovered to win for just the third time ever against Cleveland Benedictine, 47–7, and beat the University School on a rare Saturday night game.

Ross marched through the final Greater Buckeye Conference season undefeated, winning close games against Findlay, Napoleon (in overtime) and Marion Harding and then blowing out Lima Senior.

The Blue Streaks, on the other hand, were 3–2 going into the conference season, with losses to Columbus St. Charles and St. John's Jesuit. Sandusky beat Lima Senior 42–21 before getting rolled by Findlay 49–14. The Streaks then beat Harding and Napoleon, setting up a Week Ten showdown for all the marbles. A Sandusky win would give them a tie for the GBC and would likely clinch a playoff spot. A Ross win would give the Little Giants the final GBC crown outright and keep them in the hunt for a home playoff game—something that had happened just twice for Ross.

But beyond that, Ross was highly motivated at the memory of the previous year's drubbing—and the coaching staff did whatever they could to keep that memory fresh. "Every time they didn't want to do an extra squat or extra sprint, all we would say was 'thirty to nothing,' and they knew what we meant," Derek Kidwell said.

Ross threw three interceptions, and Sandusky threw two picks in the scoreless first half of the game. But the Little Giants fumbled on the opening possession of the second half, and Sandusky turned it into a touchdown by Cordney Strickland. On the ensuing drive, Ross running back Tylor Trautwein scored a touchdown to tie the game, and two minutes later, a reverse by Greg Brown gave the Little Giants the lead.

The Blue Streaks drove down and were ready to score, but Adam Miranda sacked quarterback Lucas Poggiali on fourth and goal, and

Sandusky turned the ball over on downs. With 8:44 left to play, Trautwein ran 76 yards (he gained 271 yards that night on thirty-nine carries for the Little Giants, the fifth-best single game performance in school history) for the final touchdown of the night. Ross held on to win 21–7, and minutes after the clock wound down, players and coaches had Greater Buckeye Conference Champion T-shirts.

Ross ended up tied for fourth in Division I, Region 2, and played St. John's Jesuit—one of its future rivals in the Three Rivers Athletic Conference—in a playoff game at Doyt Perry Stadium at Bowling Green State University, giving the first-round matchup the feel of a later playoff game with an ostensibly neutral site. District player of the year Cheatham Norrils was too much for the Little Giants, who lost 45–35 and dropped to 1–6 all-time in the playoffs.

Sandusky, meanwhile, snuck into the playoffs in the eighth spot in Division II, Region 6, and got its first playoff berth in twenty years, a trip to Avon against the top-seeded Eagles. But the Blue Streaks won a barnburner, 42–35, and advanced to play Maple Heights, the 2009 state runner-up. The Mustangs won in a blowout, 61–27, on the way to an undefeated season and a Division II state title.

Rob Lytle was home alone on November 20, 2010, when he started having chest pains. He called 911, and an ambulance transported him the short distance to Fremont Memorial Hospital, where he died from a heart attack eight days after his fifty-sixth birthday. There were outpourings of sympathy from the University of Michigan and the Denver Broncos, but in Fremont, he was regarded as a true Little Giant. He'd served as a coach in Fremont, became a pillar of the community (a center for the developmentally disabled is named for Lytle, who served as vice-president of the Sandusky County Board of DD) and during high school football Fridays could be found working the chain gang at Harmon Field at Don Paul Stadium.

After playing each other in the regular season finale for the forty-third time, Ross and Sandusky would turn around and play each other in the season opener the following year. For the first time as far back as anyone could remember, the Ross-Sandusky game didn't have the chill of the fall air. It was the first time in a decade that Ross and Sandusky were in the same division. After years of hovering around the cutoff mark, Ross finally dropped to Division II for the 2011 season.

Also in 2011, Strobel Field got a new look—and a new name. Thanks to donations by many, including alumnus Orlando Pace and Cedar Point amusement park, the field was now FieldTurf, and in recognition of the donations, it was now called Strobel Field at Cedar Point Stadium.

And for the first time since 1996, Ross and Sandusky were meeting as non-league opponents. Sandusky was now part of a seven-team Northern Ohio League, while Ross was a charter member of the Three Rivers Athletic Conference (TRAC), which was already being described as a "superconference."

The teams that left the Toledo City League to form the TRAC were the powers of that conference. Toledo Central Catholic was just six years removed from a Division II state championship (in a year that saw their only loss coming to Ross in Week Two) and the year before, St. John's Jesuit and Whitmer both made deep playoff runs. The Titans succumbed to the Panthers in the regional finals. Whitmer, in turn, lost to eventual state champion Lakewood St. Ed's in the state semifinals. Schools now in the TRAC had won twenty-four of the previous twenty-five Toledo City League championships.

Ross and Sandusky met in the opener at Strobel Field in 2011, and it appeared the Blue Streaks were going to christen the new turf with a score on the game's opening possession, as Sandusky set up shop on Ross's twenty-six-yard line after a sixty-five-yard kickoff return by Marquise Winston. The Blue Streaks marched down to the three-yard line but were held to a field goal attempt on fourth down, which was blocked by Marquan McDonald. The Little Giants then covered eighty yards on eight plays for the first score on the new turf, a touchdown pass by Tyler Wolf to Skylar Reffner. Wolf then ran in a two-point conversion. Sandusky then turned the ball over, and six plays later, Wolf hit McDonald for another touchdown pass to make it 14–0. The score was 14–7 after one quarter when Poggiali hit Dameyion Smith with a three-yard touchdown pass. Trent Stout scored in the second to give Ross a 20–7 halftime lead.

Then the Little Giants really started handing the ball to sophomore Jabree Lather, who picked up 196 yards on thirty-four carries, including a touchdown at the beginning of the fourth quarter. Ross rolled to a 40–28 win.

But the teams went in opposite directions after the game. Sandusky didn't lose another game during the regular season, winning the Northern Ohio League title. Strobel Field would host a home playoff game for the Blue Streaks against Tiffin Columbian. Two weeks earlier, Sandusky had edged the Tornadoes 35–34 in a league matchup, but this time, Tiffin Columbian got a 25–20 win.

Ross was 3–0 going into the TRAC season and faced St. John's Jesuit, the team that had ended their playoff season the year before. After a chippy game that saw the Titans win 35–28 in two overtimes, the Little Giants appeared to lose their bearings. Kidwell held his team back from a game-ending handshake and was suspended for the following week against Lima Senior, a 40–17 road win for Ross to bring them to 4–1. But the Little Giants then lost four of their next five to finish 5–5. Had they beaten Findlay in the season finale, the Little Giants would have probably been able to get into the playoffs with a 6–4 record, a far cry from their days in the GBC, when they could go 8–2 and sit home the first weekend in November.

In 2012, the Little Giants hosted the season opener and once again turned Jabree Lather loose on the Blue Streaks. Lather ran for 183 yards on twenty-seven carries, with a touchdown on offense and another on the opening kickoff as Ross won 52–18. It was the most points the Little Giants had ever scored on Sandusky. Lather and Kidwell gave credit to the offensive line, which controlled the line of scrimmage. Quarterback Tyler Wolf threw for three scores, two to Dylan Starks and one to Jacob Luc, and ran for another touchdown. Devante Daniels also had a rushing touchdown for Ross. For Sandusky, Lucas Will completed ten of twenty-four passes for 174 yards, including touchdowns to Mike Delk and Ben Fuller, but threw four interceptions.

The Blue Streaks stumbled through their non-league schedule, entering NOL play at 1–4. Ross, on the other hand, won the next week at Brecksville-Broadview Heights but lost to Pickerington North before going into the TRAC season. From there, Ross could win just one more league game, beating Lima Senior, and finished 3–7, equaling Sandusky's mark. Both leagues ended up having state tournament participants, as Bellevue (which beat Sandusky in the last game of the season) represented the NOL in Division III, losing in the finals to Akron St. Vincent-St. Mary. From the TRAC, Whitmer and Toledo Central Catholic advanced to the state finals, with the Irish taking the Division II crown, and the Panthers losing to Cincinnati Archbishop Moeller in the Division I finals.

The Little Giants and Blue Streaks will meet again to open the 2013 season. They have been playing each other for nearly 120 years. The rivalry has outlasted multiple conferences and endured separate leagues. The game of football literally grew up around it, with the formation of the OHSAA, the NCAA and the NFL. The two teams have been playing since before the forward pass. Sometimes, league titles and playoff berths were at stake. But there's more than a century of tradition and a heated rivalry that's always on the line.

"You talk about a great rivalry," said Bob Reiber, who served as a Sandusky assistant coach for nearly twenty years. "But it's really a great friendship."

YEAR-BY-YEAR RESULTS

1895: Sandusky 6, Fremont 0
1896: Sandusky 12, Fremont 0
1897: Fremont 18, Sandusky 0
1906: Sandusky 23, Fremont 0;
   Sandusky 5, Fremont 0
1907: Sandusky 5, Fremont 5
1908: Fremont 16, Sandusky 11;
   Sandusky win by forfeit
1909: Sandusky 11, Fremont 6
1910: Sandusky 10, Fremont 5
1912: Sandusky 37, Fremont 0
1913: Sandusky 6, Fremont 6
1914: Sandusky 35, Fremont 0
1915: Fremont won by forfeit
1916: Fremont 19, Sandusky 0
1917: Sandusky 18, Fremont 0
1918: Sandusky 32, Fremont 0
1919: Fremont 12, Sandusky 6
1920: Fremont 42, Sandusky 0
1922: Sandusky 32, Fremont 0
1923: Fremont 13, Sandusky 6
1924: Fremont 0, Sandusky 0
1925: Fremont 8, Sandusky 0
1926: Fremont 0, Sandusky 0
1927: Sandusky 2, Fremont 0

1928: Sandusky 3, Fremont 2
1929: Sandusky 14, Fremont 9
1930: Sandusky 6, Fremont Ross 6
1931: Sandusky 26, Fremont Ross 12
1932: Sandusky 33, Fremont Ross 0
1933: Sandusky 18, Fremont Ross 0
1934: Sandusky 13, Fremont Ross 9
1935: Sandusky 13, Fremont Ross 7
1936: Sandusky 13, Fremont Ross 6
1937: Sandusky 26, Fremont Ross 0
1938: Sandusky 28, Fremont Ross 6
1939: Sandusky 19, Fremont Ross 0
1940: Sandusky 46, Fremont Ross 0
1941: Fremont Ross 14, Sandusky 7
1942: Sandusky 15, Fremont Ross 6
1944: Sandusky 0, Fremont Ross 0
1945: Sandusky 14, Fremont Ross 0
1946: Fremont Ross 19, Sandusky 0
1947: Fremont Ross 13, Sandusky 0
1948: Fremont Ross 20, Sandusky 7
1949: Fremont Ross 47, Sandusky 7
1950: Sandusky 29, Fremont Ross 7
1951: Fremont Ross 19, Sandusky 14
1952: Fremont Ross 7, Sandusky 7
1953: Fremont Ross 19, Sandusky 7

1954: Sandusky 13, Fremont Ross 0
1955: Fremont Ross 20, Sandusky 6
1956: Fremont Ross 25, Sandusky 7
1957: Fremont Ross 14, Sandusky 13
1958: Sandusky 46, Fremont Ross 0
1959: Sandusky 32, Fremont Ross 26
1960: Sandusky 32, Fremont Ross 0
1961: Fremont Ross 24, Sandusky 6
1962: Sandusky 30, Fremont Ross 6
1963: Sandusky 34, Fremont Ross 0
1964: Sandusky 16, Fremont Ross 0
1965: Sandusky 54, Fremont Ross 0
1966: Sandusky 74, Fremont Ross 0
1967: Sandusky 36, Fremont Ross 6
1968: Sandusky 13, Fremont Ross 3
1969: Fremont Ross 28, Sandusky 27
1970: Sandusky 23, Fremont Ross 9
1971: Fremont Ross 32, Sandusky 0
1972: Fremont Ross 14, Sandusky 0
1973: Fremont Ross 24, Sandusky 8
1974: Fremont Ross 33, Sandusky 0
1975: Sandusky 7, Fremont Ross 6
1976: Fremont Ross 24, Sandusky 3
1977: Fremont Ross 14, Sandusky 0
1978: Sandusky 34, Fremont Ross 16
1979: Sandusky 14, Fremont Ross 14
1980: Fremont Ross 7, Sandusky 0
1981: Fremont Ross 24, Sandusky 8
1982: Sandusky 22, Fremont Ross 0
1983: Fremont Ross 7, Sandusky 0,
  regular season; Fremont Ross 7,
  Sandusky 0, playoffs
1984: Fremont Ross 14, Sandusky 0
1985: Fremont Ross 19, Sandusky 8
1986: Sandusky 16, Fremont Ross 15
1989: Fremont Ross 21, Sandusky 17
1990: Sandusky 31, Fremont Ross 0
1991: Sandusky 7, Fremont Ross 6
1992: Sandusky 35, Fremont Ross 14
1993: Fremont Ross 20, Sandusky 14
1994: Fremont Ross 46, Sandusky 7

1995: Fremont Ross 19, Sandusky
  16, OT
1996: Sandusky 24, Fremont Ross 14
1997: Fremont Ross 21, Sandusky 6
1998: Fremont Ross 49, Sandusky 28
1999: Sandusky 10, Fremont Ross 6
2000: Fremont Ross 41, Sandusky 0
2001: Fremont Ross 21, Sandusky 0
2002: Sandusky 13, Fremont Ross 0
2003: Sandusky 42, Fremont Ross 21
2004: Sandusky 21, Fremont Ross 12
2005: Fremont Ross 42, Sandusky 20
2006: Fremont Ross 49, Sandusky 6
2007: Fremont Ross 24, Sandusky 7
2008: Fremont Ross 26, Sandusky 20
2009: Sandusky 30, Fremont Ross 0
2010: Fremont Ross 21, Sandusky 7
2011: Fremont Ross 40, Sandusky 28
2012: Fremont Ross 52, Sandusky 14

BIBLIOGRAPHY

NEWSPAPERS

Cleveland Plain Dealer
Elyria Chronicle-Telegram
Eugene Register-Guard
Fremont Daily Messenger
Fremont Daily News
Fremont News-Messenger
Massillon Independent
Pittsburgh Tribune-Review
Portsmouth Times
Sandusky Register
Toledo Blade
Toledo News-Bee

BOOKS

Bray, Bill. *Fremont Ross Football, 1970–1983, The Pride Years.* Self-published, 1984.
Coughlin, Dan. *Crazy with the Papers to Prove It.* Cleveland, OH: Gray Publishing, 2010.
Kidwell, Gene. *The Sensational 60s: Sandusky High School Football.* Self-published, 1970.

Knepper, George. *Ohio and Its People*. Kent, OH: Kent State University Press, 1989.

Millisor, Justin, and Dennis Tompkins. *The Complete Fremont Ross Football Record Book, 1895–2009*. Self-published, 2010.

Oriard, Michael. *King Football*. Chapel Hill: University of North Carolina Press, 2001.

Watson, Ruth Gessner. *Historical Reflections: Fremont Public Schools 1816–1987*. Self-published, 1987.

WEBSITES

www.ohsaa.org

INTERVIEWS

Earle Bruce
Art Bucci
John Cahill
Larry Cook
Tom Hollman
Gene Kidwell
John Lewis
Chuck Lindsey
Bob Marker
Aaron Opelt
Rex Radeloff
Bob Reiber
Dick Sherman
Charles "Butch" Wagner

About the Author

V ince Guerrieri has spent the past fifteen years in newspapers, working as a news and sports reporter, copy editor and editor. He is a Youngstown native and a graduate of Bowling Green State University. Vince has worked at the *News-Messenger* since 2005 and lives in Fremont with his wife, Shannon, and their daughter, Samantha. This is his second book.